ENDORSEMEN

MW00931153

I love this book. It drew n.. ... .ight ..om ine beginning. The descriptions are vivid to the point that you will not be reading but experiencing the essence of war – its sounds, sights, tastes, smells and feelings. It is a very good description of the American Soldier.

This book can open hardened Veterans lives to the hope that awaits them in Christ who is their point-man through life's difficulties.

1st SGT. Alvin McDonald –
Retired (Special Forces) three tours of Vietnam
MACUSOG, 5th Special Forces

I have been there like your mother & sisters, and now your wife Cheryl. I was only nineteen and going to have our first son, when Calvin was called to serve our Country.

You tell it like it was (is). I know the pain and heartache you have gone through just to write *PTSD & PSALM TWENTY-THREE: Coming Up Out Of PTSD's Trench*. Just so you can help someone with PTSD, to show them they are not alone. You give them hope and peace of mind by putting down on paper what they can't even talk about.

Thank you Bob for sharing your joys and heartaches with other Veterans and their families. And thank God for Him helping you do this.

Wilma Vander Kooi
A Veteran's wife

Lots of life - much more mercy, and a heaping helping of hope.

Sgt. Calvin Vander Kooi
Recon - Vietnam
Troop B, 1st 11th Cav.; and 1st Infantry

After the hard won sacrifices of the Iraq War, its Veterans were foolishly given away in 2011. I found myself even closer to my fellow Veterans whose service in Vietnam had also been betrayed. Not only have I come to know my old friend better through his writings on PTSD, I have come to know myself better. Thank you, Bob.

Shane Morris
Special Agent, Army CID (Ret.)
Iraq, 2005–2006

What an amazing story of courage and honesty wrapped in God's gracious merciful hand! This is a work of heart, and must have been both a joy and a curse to openly share your thoughts, feelings and actions of war in Vietnam.

May many souls be challenged, comforted and encouraged reading this, your third book. To God be the glory!! May you and Cheryl be blessed as you continue to recover.

Sharon Moss
Retired Nurse

Robert, like many of us, left a home filled with God's eternal love and was immersed into a hellish world of killing, death and dying. Robert's faith and insight allowed him courage and hope to survive. While his faith was strong, the eating effect of all the previous killing & loss created a confusion that could not be shaken off. Forty to fifty years looking for the light – Scholten's book is evidence of his undying faith and hope for peace and wholeness.

LT. Truman Hays, (Special Forces) two tours of Vietnam
502 S.F.
3rd Bgd, 25th Inf. Div.

ROBERT SCHOLTEN

PTSD
&PSALM
TWENTY-THREE
COMING UP OUT OF PTSD's TRENCH

WESTBOW
PRESS®
A DIVISION OF THOMAS NELSON
& ZONDERVAN

This book is a work of non-fiction. Unless otherwise noted, the author
and the publisher make no explicit guarantees as to the accuracy of
the information contained in this book and in some cases, names of
people and places have been altered to protect their privacy.

Scripture taken from the New King James Version. Copyright © 1979, 1980,
1982 by Thomas Nelson, Inc. Used by permission. All rights reserved.

Scripture taken from the King James Version of the Bible.

WestBow Press books may be ordered through booksellers or by contacting:

WestBow Press
A Division of Thomas Nelson & Zondervan
1663 Liberty Drive
Bloomington, IN 47403
www.westbowpress.com
1 (866) 928-1240

Because of the dynamic nature of the Internet, any web addresses or
links contained in this book may have changed since publication and
may no longer be valid. The views expressed in this work are solely those
of the author and do not necessarily reflect the views of the publisher,
and the publisher hereby disclaims any responsibility for them.

Any people depicted in stock imagery provided by Thinkstock are
models, and such images are being used for illustrative purposes only.
Certain stock imagery © Thinkstock.

ISBN: 978-1-5127-2805-7 (sc)
ISBN: 978-1-5127-2807-1 (hc)
ISBN: 978-1-5127-2806-4 (e)

Library of Congress Control Number: 2016901191

Print information available on the last page.

WestBow Press rev. date: 02/01/2016

CONTENTS

DEDICATION

I dedicate *PTSD & PSALM TWENTY – THREE: Coming Up Out Of PTSD's Trench* in part to:

Dr. Cynthia Dunn, who has helped hundreds of Veterans deal with their PTSD symptoms, and guide them out of despair into hope, of which I am one. Dr. Dunn is Dr. Dee in the "Introduction To Post Traumatic Stress Disorder" of *PSALM TWENTY FIVE & PTSD*; of which I published through Tate Publishing & Enterprises;

My fellow PTSD sufferers and their families & friends;

My family who has loved me unconditionally, regardless of what I have put them through;

Jackson County Veterans Outreach in Jackson County, Kentucky.

FOREWORD

A Veteran's Perspective:

Mr. Scholten's book offers a very unique insight into the world and heart of the Vietnam War. All too often, we as Americans have only scratched the surface of what it takes to survive our daily lives. Robert Scholten was an average American doing just that when duty called. With unshakable faith in the Lord, he found himself thousands of miles away from home sitting in a musty bunker in a strange land facing the unknown.

As a fellow Veteran (OIF1) the struggles of being away from home and its comforts, and often time the boredom of being a soldier can be just as hard – if not harder. Couple these with the struggle the individual feels in maintaining a shred of personal identity and faith, and you got yourself the recipe for a hardened Veteran.

Mr. Scholten's book is a great read for anyone looking for a great story; and a must read for any Veteran suffering with PTSD, or not, no matter your religious preference. Mr. Scholten's insights and relationship with PTSD and his path to recovery will hit home and speak to your heart.

Spc.4 (Ret.) Ferguson, Loren S.,
Combat Medic, U.S. Army 2-70th AR. 1st AD.

A Civilian's Perspective:

Thank you for the opportunity to proof read your newest manuscript. I may have missed things due to being absorbed with reading your stories. Your descriptions are powerful. I often imagined I was <u>seeing</u> your story rather than reading it. The stories that stood out the most to me are <u>Night</u>, <u>Death</u>, <u>Comfort</u>, and <u>Dwelling</u>.

Your words are mirrors to so many things I've heard from Veterans – they will be very validating and inspirational.

Kelly Gauble, PhD
Licensed Psychologist
PTSD Clinical Team
Department of Veterans Affairs
Lexington, Kentucky

PREFACE

PTSD (Post Traumatic Stress Disorder) has seemingly become a buzz word of late. But, it is much more. It is a reality birthed in trauma and nurtured in isolation. A reality that eventually bares destructive fruit filled with acid, which eats away at everything that gives life meaning.

War haunts many of those who have been or are caught up in its madness. PTSD is such a haunting. It is real. It is all too real for all too many Veterans of all too many wars.

PTSD eventually caught up to me and hijacked my family in the process. My loving family watched me unravel before their eyes. An unraveling which left them bewildered and sometimes scared. They didn't have a clue of what was happening within my brain that was rewired by long term PTSD. Nor did they know what was happening down deep in my soul.

Nearly 40 years after my tour of Vietnam my struggle came to a climax. This led me to being admitted into the Lexington, Kentucky's Veterans Administration's six week in-house PTSD Rehabilitation Program in November 2007. While there I was totally out of my element. The temptation to leave was ever present, but I stuck it out. Years later I am still under their care - for which I am grateful.

Those who do not suffer with PTSD may find this book rather difficult to read. It does not flow normally like most books, rather it is choppy at times. We with PTSD live in two worlds simultaneously – that of the past and present.

Our lives are filled with flashbacks, nightmares, isolation, and a host of other degrading things. If these things are left unchecked, they will destroy relationships and sometimes life itself.

PTSD & PSALM TWENTY – THREE: Coming Up Out Of PTSD's Trench is written in a way that PTSD sufferers will identify with it. It is a view of PTSD from the inside looking outward.

Welcome to my world.

TERMINOLOGY

Track capitalized indicates Duster.
Track not capitalized indicates the tracks on the Duster.

A.I.T. = Advanced Individual Training
ARVN = South Vietnamese Army
Breech = The back end of a cannon or gun
Charlie = Viet Cong
Claymore = antipersonnel mine, filled with hundreds of small steel balls, with a killing range of 50 meters
C.O. = Commanding Officer
Cobra gunship = AH-1G HUEY Helicopter
C-rations = Combat rations consisting of canned meals for Combatants in the field
DEROS = Date Eligible For Return From Oversees
Duster = M42A1 self-propelled automatic twin 40mm antiaircraft gun Track
Fire Base = Small or large, temporary or fixed, artillery complexes
Free Fire Zone / Kill Zone = No permission needed to shoot to kill
K.P. Kitchen Patrol / Police = Cleaning & working in the mess-hall
L.Z. = Landing Zone
NVA = North Vietnam Army

O.D. = Olive Drab (official color of Army vehicles & equipment)

PX = Post Exchange – market / store

Starlight Scope = A night vision scope that uses light from the stars and moon to illuminate targets for the viewer / guard

Quad Fifty = 50 caliber machinegun gun truck (with 4 mounted guns)

V.C. = Viet Cong

Wire = Razor wire strung out around a perimeter

What is a Duster?

Look it up online "Dusters in the Vietnam War." There will be many sites to look at, including the "National Dusters, Quads, Searchlights Association."

You will find it helpful to see what a Duster looks like before reading beyond the Introduction of this book, PTSD & PSALM TWENTY-THREE: Coming Up Out Of PTSD's Trench.

INTRODUCTION

Out of the corner of my eye I see a Viet Cong sneaking up on me with a drawn knife. Instinctively pivoting my body's weight upon the bottom of my right foot, I turn - chopping the weapon out of his hand. I sense his dread and my rush for survival. It's him or me. I have to complete the maneuver.

It is beyond my control as all my training and combat experience kick in to finish the job. I can feel his breath, which means I have less than a second and only inches between life and death. I want to close my eyes but can't - lest I miss the mark and he wins and I die.

"Robert," my wife of 38 years yells as I face her in the kitchen of our home in the Appalachian Mountains of Southeastern Kentucky. There we stand inches apart in two different worlds within a loving home strained by Post Traumatic Stress Disorder. Cheryl's eyes are the size of saucers and her lovely face flushed of all color. My eyes are focused and my face stern.

As we stand looking at each other, all I can say is, "You startled me." Cheryl is speechless - frozen in fear.

"I suppose I better make an appointment to see Doctor Dunn," I softly say - in a broken voice of disbelief of what could have happened. "Yes! You better," Cheryl says as she backs up from me, guiding herself with her hand on the kitchen island overflowing with stuff.

Stuff. So much stuff yet to deal with that neither of us knew had to come to the surface. Our lives could have been transformed into something resembling our disarranged kitchen island. A family forever changed. A murderer standing over his dead wife. Over what? A pan! A lousy pan.

Cheryl was bringing me a pan, which she thought I would use to make breakfast. Instead, she stepped into my world of PTSD in which I am constantly on guard. The VA psychologists call it "hyper vigilance." We combat Veterans with PTSD call it "survival."

Time has moved on since that episode in 2013, but it remains a constant reminder to Cheryl of a time she was paralyzed by raw fear. It remains a concern to me of Cheryl's wondering of a future repeat.

We walk side by side and hand in hand together – two hearts knit together by love and trust.[1] We, however, walk in two different worlds never losing sight of each other. It is faith, hope and love that holds us together and keeps us close.[2]

Welcome to our world. Some of you will instantly understand and identify with the previous and that which will follow. Some of you will struggle to understand – if so, thank God, for you do not have PTSD.

Chapter 1

NIGHT

It is night. It is dark. There is nothing in comparison to the darkness of night in war. To a combatant it is dreadful, because nights are owned by the enemy. To a Veteran, it takes time to readjust to nights in the civilian world. It is an adjustment that comes hard—if it comes at all.

I have just met my crew members, some of whom looked upon me with suspicion. They are a tight-knit group who learned mutual trust and comradeship under extreme stress that would snap a civilian like a dry twig under a horse's hoof.

I arrive at my Section's location around noon in September of 1970. Shortly thereafter, I am led to the perimeter and introduced to my chariot of war—a Duster. It is a twenty-five-ton open-turret Track armed with twin 40 millimeter cannons that spits out 240 rounds per minute. I am horrified at the thought of being a crew member of such a killing machine. It is not used against aircraft but against enemy ground troops.

After a quick introduction to its capabilities, I am led to a bunker. It stands about six feet tall and is surrounded by sand-filled 40mm ammo cans stacked two deep and two high, with layers of sandbags on top of them. The roof is comprised of thick wood beams, covered with corrugated metal, and topped with multiple layers of sandbags. There are no windows and only one narrow door, through which I enter a dark, close-quartered, damp, musty, rat-infested world called home. (I will soon discover this is a Hilton compared to other places farther out in the boonies.)

So much to learn in such a short time. I am assigned a bunk in the bunker and told to memorize its close quarters, including who sleeps in which bunks.

My Squad Leader tells me to have everything of importance within reach for a second's notice. Nothing short of this is acceptable. He continues, "You will pull two two-hour guard shifts and be responsible to wake your replacements. And if we receive incoming, you will be on the perimeter in a minute or less. Now go count off the steps."

A narrow slit of light shines through the bunker's door, illuminating the floor and creating an early atmosphere of shadows floating through a sunken world totally foreign to my senses. A few nights earlier, I was back home in my bed—inside my bedroom and inside my family's home. Now I have only a couple of hours to pull myself together for my first night in war with crew members I do not know.

After unpacking my duffel bag, I sit on my bunk and drop my head into my hands, praying for strength and courage.[3] My hands are cold even though it is hot and muggy. I feel drops of sweat dripping down my back and forming channels for further beads of perspiration to follow. Now my feet are trembling in my jungle boots that are tapping the floor.

Pressing my right hand against my jungle fatigues' shirt pocket, I feel a small New Testament Bible. I clench it through the pocket and reflect on Psalm 23—for surely I am in the valley of the shadow of death.

The glimmer of light on the bunker floor is retreating toward the door, leaving darkness and uncertainty in its wake. As the one-room bunker darkens, my eyes try adjusting to the new world taking its place. I take a quick inventory of my space, noting where my rifle, ammo, and helmet, along with other essentials, are located. Everything I have is new compared to the scrubby clothing, boots, and gear of my fellow crew members. However, our weapons are all well-kept, ready for use at a moment's notice.

The darker it becomes, the keener my senses become. I'm bombarded by smells. The ever-present mildew and mold assault my nose, as does the smoke from my fellow crew members' cigarettes. Up from the dirty plywood floor come the musty odors of the ground beneath it, which are joined by the stench of moisture-saturated sandbags surrounding us. Then, stuffing this place with eleven GIs changes the atmosphere altogether.

The bunk is creaking beneath my weight as I move forward to rise. Its squeaky noise quickly vanishes within this damp, hollow, fortified dwelling. Pushing myself up off the bunk, I feel the poncho liner that is the closest thing to a sheet that I'll have for the rest of my tour in Vietnam. My stomach churns with disgust and hunger.

Hunger. I haven't eaten since this morning back at the base camp. In exiting the bunker, I wonder where the mess hall is located. I cannot see or smell it. *That's strange*, I think. *I ought to smell the aroma of cooked food.* Nothing.

"Hey, what are you looking for?" a fellow crew member asks me.

"The mess hall," I reply.

The guy laughs, calling me a cherry. "There isn't a mess hall here. Go to the Track for supper," he says while shaking his head. That is my introduction to C-rations.

Walking to the Track (Duster), my stomach is empty while my mind is full of questions and thoughts that only time can answer. If I live that long.

A slight breeze cools today's heat as night falls upon us. The Duster still radiates with today's heat as I touch it. My senses explode within me. My God, what have I gotten into?

Standing there, frozen in bewilderment, I can smell the caked-on dirt in the tracks, sprockets, and fenders of the Duster. Then, the drifting smells of fuel, oil, grease, and gun oil overtake me like an ungodly sacrifice. Now I can smell the hard rubber road pads in the tracks that make this war chariot ride smoother. What's this? As darkness falls I notice something new—sounds. Everything starts changing, as does my confidence. I am truly in the valley of the shadow of death. I pray for strength and courage as my ears adjust to nighttime sounds that are totally different from morning and midday. The night is anything but quiet, as nocturnal bugs, birds, and animals fill the darkness with their sounds. It's eerie to me—as is the thought that we are surrounded by enemy, with only a few strands of wire between us. Thank God there are trip flares and claymores within the wire.

Then it hits me, we (Dusters) are the first line of defense—they have to go through us to get to those we are protecting. I didn't sign up for this, but here I am. My heart starts racing, but I calm it down through prayer and meditating on Scripture. However, the reality of this place cuts them short. I am in a battle within a war.

Returning to the bunker, I quickly turn to face the Duster and the wire again. Where is everything I was just looking at? The elephant grass is disappearing, as are the river and trees beyond. Climbing up on the duster for a better view complicates matters. Chills fill my spine as I stiffen my shoulders. In a matter of hours, I will be up on this Duster, gazing into darkness, looking for any movement, and listening for anything out of place. "Willies" replace the chills.

Climbing down off the Duster, I walk toward the bunker's fading silhouette. My eyes are straining to keep the bunker in sight. Each step I take is registering in my brain and echoing in my ears. Arriving at the bunker, I touch the sandbags to steady myself in the doorway; in doing so, I find my mind filled with a host of new feelings and emotions, pushing out the comforting words of Psalm 23.

Leaving one world outside, I enter another. A dim electric lightbulb illuminates the inside just enough to let me see the cots and makeshift tables and shelves. Everything everyone owns is stacked on these small tables and shelves and narrow cots, a duffle-bag's worth for each of us. My mind wanders back home to an overflowing closet and chest of drawers inside a spacious bedroom—and inside a two-story home. It is a home in which a grieving mother and two anxious sisters are waiting for letters postmarked from Vietnam.

The chatter in the bunker is joined by various forms of music from portable cassette players, along with the distinct sounds of preparing M16 ammo clips. The atmosphere is heavy with breathing, coughing, yawning GIs preparing for short sleep periods interrupted by guard duty. I wonder how sleep will come my way with all this racket. Will the music and talking extend into the night? Will the dim lightbulb remain on like a child's reassuring nightlight? Will I have enough time for prayer and devotions before exhaustion overtakes me? Will there be incoming? If so, will I survive? Will I be able to function as a crew member, with men I do not know on a Track I have never seen before this afternoon?

Pondering these questions on the edge of my bed, I start wondering who slept here before and what became of them. Where were they from? What were they like? Did they make it through their tours?

Sliding my body onto the narrow cot, I let down the mosquito net, swatting at the flying blood suckers trapped inside it with me. Trapped! I feel trapped.[4] My mind wanders back home but is immediately brought back when I am informed of guard duty in two hours. Two hours!

The noisy bunker slowly becomes quiet except for the creaking bunks under the tossing men trying to find comfortable positions of rest. I wonder what they are wondering. I do not even know all their names yet—and they definitely know nothing about me. Shaking my head while swatting at the buzzing sounds, I pray for strength and courage—and for my family back home and for my new family: these men. I meditate on the Scriptures, trying to draw back from memory that which I learned in church, Sunday school, youth groups, and at home. These push out fear from within and replace it with peace.[5]

There's a rhythm of sounds that act like a lullaby: men breathing and snoring and grunting, cots creaking, bugs buzzing, and my heart beating. Laying on my back, with eyes wide open, I make mental note of where the bunker's door is and the Duster beyond. My knife & flak jacket are under my thin pillow. My helmet and bandoleer of ammo clips are on a small table next to my bed. My M16 rifle is between the cot and table.

My body tenses up as I hear the footsteps of someone entering the bunker. Am I ready for this – my first watch on guard duty in war? My mind instantly reflects upon Scriptures pertaining to being on guard and watching.[6] I cannot see the guy, but hear his footsteps walking towards another bunk.

Sounds carry in darkness, creating mental pictures colored with emotions and feelings. These in turn hang in one's heart.

I hear a creaking cot followed by sounds I have never heard before, thus a new picture in my heart. I hear a man walking out into the night as another man lays on a cot shrouded in darkness. His cot creaks as he tries finding a comfortable position before being awoken in another two hours. I ask myself, "How does one get sleep in this place?" Unbeknown to me, this is the beginning of a sleep disorder I will take home.

My mind is filled with thoughts. My heart is filled with emotions. My body is filled with adrenaline. Sleep does not come easily with such a mixture. In fact, it doesn't come at all. I want to sleep but it does not come - so I rest instead. I can feel every breath and hear every mosquito. I wonder if the other guys hear me breathing and swatting at insects. I pray in the midst of this, realizing God knows where I'm at and what I'm facing.[7]

My eyelids defy my adrenaline filled body by becoming heavy and eventually closing. Once closed to this bunkered life my mind opens to a dream life. Dreams of my family back home and of my youth and of my military experiences thus far, are creating a weird motion picture effect in my spirit. I'm lost in this maze of emotional pictures, until jolted awake by the presence of someone looming over me. Standing there, in the darkness, is the guy I am to replace on guard duty. Tapping my bunk he says, "It's your watch dude."

A moan comes up from my soul surprising me but not him who stood by my cot. Rising up and twisting my body I push up the mosquito net forcing myself out of bed. Standing there, I try to gather my wits before leaving this dark place to enter another darkness - a darkness filled with uncertainties I never faced before.

Pulling out the flak jacket from underneath my pillow I slip my arms into it and zip up the zipper. Recalling the earlier unknown sounds, I realize they are the flak jacket's zipper and the gathering up of a rifle and ammo. Now, I'm making those same noises upon leaving the bunker.

Whispering a prayer I enter the darkness of night[8] that is unlike any other I've ever experienced. Adjusting my eyes to it, I try locating the Duster while walking toward the perimeter. Once again each step I take is registering in my brain and echoing in my ears.

The night air caresses my face while my ears take in all the strange sounds of nighttime Vietnam. I'm no longer in Illinois! I'm no longer in America. As the Duster comes into view I know that all thoughts of home must be pushed out.

Reaching the Duster, I climb aboard to join a fellow crew member on guard duty. The night sounds are deafening and eerie. He doesn't say anything. I say, "My name is Bob." "Quiet! You fool," is his response. "Don't give our position away," he whispers. The reality of where I'm at hits me dead center.

Chapter 2

GUARD DUTY

I hear every sound, including my beating heart. My brain, like a computer, tries analyzing all the strange new sounds. My mind attempts to create pictures in my head of all the noise makers. My overloaded nervous system sends mixed messages to all my organs, which in turn catapults me into hyper alertness. Man, I'm flying and I'm not on any drugs, but my body is saturated with adrenaline.

Being on guard duty for less than five minutes and this is happening to me! What will two hours bring? Pausing in thought, *I wonder what 363 nights of this stuff will do to me.* My entire body shakes at the thought. I hope my fellow guard does not hear my rattling bones and clicking teeth.

Deep from within my soul rises a prayer, "God help me."[9] I prayed before. I come from a heritage of prayer. But, now gloom fights for dominance in my heart as I face an unseen enemy in a darkness blacker than any I have experienced. I cannot let it happen: knowing if it does my faith will crumble and with it my sanity. The thought of such a life in such a place for such a long time nearly bursts my heart with grief. Further prayer pushes back despair to allow peace of heart and mind to regain their proper places.[10]

This internal battle seems to be raging for hours, but in reality it's been seconds. My eyes return to their wartime duties, as do my ears, as does my mind. My entire body follows. Once again I'm engulfed in the reality of a war that can take my life at any moment. Sitting in the open turret of this Track with my fellow guard, I join him in defying the odds of death - hoping to face one more day. One less day of our tours. One day closer to our homes. I tell myself, "Stop it," realizing thoughts of home, or of getting out of this place, while on guard duty is dangerous and could get me and others killed. Nearly two hours still to pull. This is going to be harder than I ever imagined.

Nothing prepared me for guard duty in war. Nothing prepared me for the gruesome reality of war. Nothing prepared me for tonight. But here I am.

Readjusting my senses to the task at hand, I watch and listen. Peering into the darkness I try locating the razor sharp wire that separates us from the enemy. I know it's there along with the trip-flares and claymores. Finally, some moonlight filters through the cloudy night sky revealing the wire and some of what is beyond. The moonlight and high humidity and mist add to the eeriness that shrouds me like a damp wool blanket.

The various shades of gray hiding the rich colors of Vietnam in a blanket of darkness begin playing tricks with my mind. I strain my eyes to see beyond the wire while paying attention to all the surrounding sounds. Then there's the ever presence of the ghostly enemy that can inch themselves up to my position. I am facing more enemies than Viet Cong. I am facing night itself, fears, anxieties, doubts, tiredness, thoughts of home and God forbid – sleep.

Snapping my mind back to attention I focus on the sounds. Now sounds are playing tricks in my mind and heart. I am on an emotional rollercoaster that beats any manmade one. This one however can kill me.

Sensing my nervousness my fellow guard whispers, "All the chirping insects and birds are our friends – as long as you hear them Charlie isn't near. Get ready for trouble if they stop."

That makes sense, I think. Now I'm hoping the noise doesn't end. So I start focusing more on watching than listening.

Then he continues, "Keep alert, because Charlie can crawl so slowly and quietly that he can trick our chirping friends out there."

My heart skips a beat at this added information I didn't want to hear. "Thanks," I whisper back while praying for strength and courage and alertness to make it through this watch, and my second one later tonight. Looking at my wristwatch, I'm shocked at the reality of how slow time ticks by on guard duty. I have been here for only fifteen minutes. An hour and forty-five minutes remaining.

"Stop it," I tell myself knowing I must keep totally alert, pushing back desires for rest and sleep. *The bunker is a far better place than this open turret I'm sitting in,* I think to myself. "Stop feeling sorry for yourself," I say in my heart thanking God I am not out here alone. The thought of being alone on guard duty sends chills down my spine.

Leaning to my left, I feel the thinly quarter inch armored turret's edge against my arm. The cold steel comes up to my shoulder, leaving my neck and head exposed. I yearn for my heavy armored 52 ton M60 Tank. Leaning to my right, the breech acts as an arm rest. Little do I know at the time that my head will be bombarded by percussion waves from this rapid firing weapon. Nor that I will leave Vietnam with hearing loss, constant ringing in my ears, and a persistent headache.

This turret I'm sitting in is very cramped, considering there will be four men in here when we roll out on a mission. My fellow guard steps out of the turret to sit on the twin cannons' barrels pointing toward the perimeter. He leans against the front shield that protects the breeches and stretches his legs out on the barrels. He is relaxing while I am wishing I can be more like him. He has been here for months while I have been here for hours.

He has survived countless missions and firefights while I haven't experienced any such things.

I whisper, "Hey you can get shot sitting out there." To which he replies, "Cherry - it don't mean nothin'." I wonder about such a strange remark. Surely it means something! Life must mean something.[11] One's life must mean something. I know mine does. Surely he must value his life.[12] Little do I know at the time about the sad reality behind this strange saying of, "It don't mean nothn'." Nor, do I know about the constant spiritual battle I will fight within my soul, to keep myself from totally embracing this saying's mad heritage anchored deep in this strange war unlike many others.

War is war. But what is Vietnam? Is it a war or a conflict? A conflict is something that can be walked away from. A war is something that must be won at all costs. "God, what have I gotten into?" I ask both myself and God. I search my mind and heart for answers but come up with none. The thought of a year in this place makes me grasp my M16 rifle that is leaning up against my chest. This in turn gets me to meditate on God's Word which is symbolized as a sword.[13] "It's a sword for a reason," I whisper out loud.

"What did you say?" my fellow guard asks.

"Nothing, just thinking out loud," I reply.

Regaining my senses for their duties here in the night, I watch and listen - taking everything in like a sponge.

Resisting looking at my wristwatch, I keep gazing into the night trying to focus in on objects beyond the wire. The free-fire zone (kill-zone) just beyond the wire is free of any living thing. Agent Orange makes sure of that. Beyond that the tall elephant grass sways in a gentle breeze.

I never seen such tall grass. It is unbelievably high. Much higher than our Track. Thus anybody or anything can hide in it. I cannot see the river and tree line beyond the grass. I know they are there. That is when fear starts knocking at my heart's door. "They're out there and they are coming for you," it sneers. At the same time the Lord is knocking at my heart's door saying, "*Peace, be still, and know I am God.*"[14] Who do I believe? The choice is easy: He who never forsakes me[15] and holds me in the palm of His hand.[16]

Finally, after what seemed like an hour or more, I raise my arm to see what time it is. "Nuts, just 30 minutes has passed," I say to myself so loud I thought for sure my fellow guard heard me.

Getting thirsty I reach for my canteen. "Nuts." I left my canteen that is connected to my web/utility-belt in the bunker. I also left my knife. What else did I forget, I wonder? Now I am thinking about how thirsty I am. Come to think of it, I am also getting hungry.

"I got a lot to learn," I say to myself.

"What did you say Cherry?"

"I left my canteen back in the bunker. I got a lot to learn," I reply.

"Yes you do, and you best start now. When my replacement comes, quick go get your canteen and anything else you need," he says while never dropping his gaze before him.

Anything else I need. There is a lot I need. A "Three Musketeer bar," a "Coke" and potato chips. Forget the chips, they make noise. Now I am really getting hungry, because I have none of these luxuries. Now, I begin thinking about when and where I can stock up on them. The more I think the more hungry I become.

"Stop it," I tell myself knowing I must keep focusing on watching and listening. However, simple pleasures such as snacks, television, rest, driving a car, going to a friend's or relative's home, attending church, or sitting on a back porch start cascading into my heart. They bring a smile to my face and a sigh from my spirit. They also take me away from what I must be doing.

I wonder if everyone goes through this. And if so, how long it takes to conquer it. This gets me thinking about what will happen if we are attacked tonight. What the heck will I do since I have never been on such a guard duty before? Will I be a gunner or a loader or go down to the wire?

Here on my first night of guard duty, it comes down to answering a dreadful question, "Will I be able to kill another human being?" Snuff the very essence of life from a person? How will I handle it? Better yet, how will it handle me? God have mercy, I am in Vietnam. I am not alone. Men and women have been asking these questions for centuries, and will continue to ask them to the end of time."

Taking a deep breath I let the air out slowly nearly forgetting to breathe again. Another deep breath followed by a long sigh. My chest feels trapped in my flak jacket that is heavy and tight. My jacket looks so new compared to my fellow crew members' jackets. I wonder what mine will look like in a month's time. A year is just too much to think about.

"Thank you Lord for this here jacket and helmet and for my new boots and clothes and field jacket, and everything else I have." I have much to be thankful for and much to live for.[17] Life is worth the living - even in war.[18] Easy to say with such little time under my belt. How little do I know what I will be facing in months to come!

Time passes slowly - but it passes. I hear approaching footsteps from behind me. A fellow crew member is arriving to replace the other guard. He gets to go back to the bunker while I still have an hour to pull. At least it is just one hour now. Hopefully the coming hour will be just as uneventful as the previous.

I am given a few minutes to get my canteen, which I do. This water from this canteen tastes terrible compared to the fresh water back home. It has a chemical aroma and flavor. But, it is wet. I gulp some water down, screwing on the canteen's lid afterwards, then placing it in its canvas case attached to my belt.

My belt: it has a canteen, a red lensed flashlight, knife, a canvas ammo clip pouch, and a medical pouch. Thinking about the belt, I hope I never have to use the knife, nor my medical kit, nor the extra ammo clip. This gets me thinking about the "*armor of God*"[19] Christians symbolically wear in their spiritual conflicts in a world gone insane with sin.[20]

Climbing back on the Duster I take my place in the turret again. The new guard stands up and says, "Hang on." I wonder what he means by that. He walks forward on the left fender lowering himself into the driver's hatch. Shortly thereafter, I hear a loud pop followed by a roar and the clicking of tracks passing through sprockets. He backs up our Duster and moves it elsewhere on the perimeter.

Afterwards he tells me this is done to throw off Charlie, so they cannot zero in on our Track with rockets or mortars. Once again the reality of this place hits me dead center.

Forty-five minutes left before I can go back to the bunker. The second hour seems to pass faster. I start hoping my next two - hour watch will go by as fast as the second hour of this one.

Now that we moved, I need to refocus in on all the different sights that stretch before us beyond the wire. Adding to my bewilderment is the rising mist that by morning will be a thick layer of fog. By the time I have focused in on the wire and some of that which lays beyond, my shift comes to a close. I'm told to leave ten minutes early so I can guide my replacement back to the Duster.

I don't want this responsibility, but it is mine. My fellow guard points me in the direction of the bunker and says, "Get some rest, you will be back in two hours."

"My Lord, two hours! I can sleep for a week" echoes in my heart.

Once again each step I take is registering in my brain and echoing in my ears while walking back to the bunker. Entering in, I hope I'm waking the right guy for guard duty. The last thing I want to do is get someone mad at me my first night.

Tapping his shoulder, he jerks up jumping to his feet coming face to face with me. "Don't do that again," he says.

"Do what?" I ask.

"Touch me in the middle of the night. You are lucky I didn't have my knife in my hand. You tap the bed post (that which holds up the mosquito netting)," he said.

This shakes me up more than the previous two hours. With a shaky voice I tell him that the Duster moved and I am to take him to it.

"Forget it. I'll find it. It don't mean nothin' anyway. Go get some sleep. You will relieve me in two hours," he tells me as he gathers up his gear.

I collapse dead tired into my bunk - flak jacket and all.

Chapter 3

SLEEP

Sleep does not come this first night in which I pull my first guard duty, with another watch coming in two hours. I am dead tired, but adrenaline and a fully active mind push back any efforts sleep tries to advance in my body.

I am enclosed by thick layers of sandbags on a small compound encircled by a few strands of wire surrounded by the enemy. I've been tired before but nothing like this. I murmur to myself in the belly of this bunker, "My God, my first night with my Unit and I'm this tired. What is to become of me?"

Sleep is needed before my next guard duty in two hours. Two hours and counting. 120 minutes ticking down second by second all too quickly. My night is divided into two hour segments. Gone are good nights of sleep back home. Nice dreams are gone too. I am in a nightmare that will last for months on end.

The only sure way I know of relaxing myself is by meditating on the Scriptures and praying. Reaching through my mosquito netting I retrieve my Bible from the small stand next to my bunk. It is a thick black leather bound Bible with silver edged pages that my maternal grandmother gave me a few years earlier.

She was a woman of faith and prayer who deeply loved the Lord, His Word and me. We lived with her. She said to my father, "Bert, you bring home the bacon & love and I'll supply the house." My father, a WWII Veteran, didn't have a high paying job. However, he did his best as a carpenter in a steel mill on Chicago's Southside.

Upon retrieving the Bible memories of my family came with it. I am not ready for the onslaught of thoughts and feelings that bombard me emotionally. I see my grandmother's smiling face and hear her say, "Remember Bobby, I'm praying for you." I see my mother and sisters' faces moments before boarding the airplane in O'Hare Airport on my way to Vietnam. I also recall my father on his deathbed in Chicago's VA Hospital saying, "I hate that war," as he watches the evening news on a flickering black and white television screen.

My grandmother and father died a few months apart, less than two years prior to my coming down on levy for Vietnam. Good thing! My being in Vietnam nearly killed my mother. Lord only knows what would have happened to my father and grandmother. Looking back forty-five years later, I have to admit that first night with my Unit had major impacts on my life.

I put my helmet under the pillow and scoot myself up in a makeshift reclining position. With flashlight in one hand and open Bible in the other, I begin meditating and praying.

Reading comes hard to me, but I struggle on bringing to memory Bible stories heard and learned both in church and home. I chuckle down deep thinking about how I tried getting out of going to Sunday school, church, catechism,[21] youth group and other religious events as a child and young teen. Now, I thank God for those years.

After reading Psalm 23 and 25 I replace my helmet under the pillow with my flak jacket and Bible and knife. What a combination.

Staring into the darkness I begin meditating and praying as my eyelids grow heavy. I am praying for my extended family and friends back home, and for my crew members here in this dreadful place. I do not know all their names yet, nor the names of those in my "Section." There are eleven of us. Two crews (Squads) of five men and one "Chief" between us serving on two sister Tracks.

"*Two sister Tracks,*" I think out loud. I cannot help but think of my two sisters' back home thinking about me here in Vietnam. Two sisters of flesh and blood thousands of miles away, and two sisters of steal and weaponry only yards away. Two sisters back home watching newscasts of the war, and two sisters of war ready to take human life in that war. Two sisters praying for their brother's life, and their brother praying he doesn't have to take a life. What a mishmash.

Sleep still avoids me as I try thinking on different things. *I'm thinking too much*, I think to myself. I am trapped within a trap with one of three ways out: end of my yearlong tour, wounded or death. I am not alone in this trap. I am joined by my fellow crew and Section members, and all other Service Members here in Vietnam.

It is night. It is cold. It is miserable. It is less than twenty-four hours that I have been on this compound with people I don't know, surrounded by people wanting me dead. I still do not know what is expected of me. I am hoping it is driving the Duster. I want to be the driver rather than being up in the open turret of this killing machine.

All these thoughts and prayers and Scriptures start mingling with previous war movies and television shows I watched in the past - the not too distant past. Now, I am wide awake in the middle of the night in the middle of a war. What a mixture.

I cannot sleep now if I want too. Laying here just hours into my "war" I wonder what is in store for me in the days, weeks and months to come. This wondering is cut short by a dripping noise next to my bunk. I feel my bunk wiggle followed by hearing a guy saying, "It's your watch. You will need your field jacket and poncho."

Gathering up my gear I put on my helmet, field jacket, flak jacket and finally slip into my rain poncho. Exiting the bunker I have all my essentials: knife, rifle, ammo, canteen, flashlight, and Bible. What a combination.

"God, it is cold out here," I say to myself as I walk through the driving rain pelting my poncho. Walking toward the Duster through the mud puddles I hear the rain on my raingear, smell the rain & mud and taste the rain dripping off my face into my mouth. Two hours of this. What a sight.

Arriving at the Duster I climb aboard to begin my second shift of guard duty. There is no shelter from the rain that is soaking me and my fellow guard. These ponchos are a joke in this drenching rain unlike any I've experienced before. I am tired, cold, wet and miserable in the beginning minutes of my watch. What will the next two hours bring? More unending rain makes the night darker and more dangerous, in that Charlie can sneak up on us.

Pushing out all thoughts of home, I look into the rainy night seeing only a few yards ahead of me. I am hoping the trip-flares and claymores will do their jobs. I'm shivering with goosebumps on my goosebumps - thinking the whole while that there is something wrong with this picture. This second watch is going to be harder to endure than my previous one. There is nothing I can do but endure it. The foul weather keeps me wide awake. Once again I cannot sleep even if I wanted too. All I hear is the driving rain smacking the Duster and our ponchos.

The heavy rain eventually gives way to a soaking rain. I'm still miserable, but there is a blessing – I begin hearing the night sounds of Vietnam. However, the darkness is eerie as ever.

My elbows are on my knees and my chin is resting on my clasped hands. My M16 is laying against my chest as I gaze out into the darkness. Time means nothing as it ticks on minute by minute. Like it or not, I am here. Regardless of my thoughts and beliefs, I have the responsibility of keeping those I'm guarding safe at all costs – including my life.

Finally, we hear approaching footsteps slushing through the mud puddles toward our Track from behind us. "About time," my fellow guard whispers as his replacement climbs up into the Duster. Nothing is said as the switch is made. I wonder if this is normal or if it is because of the lousy weather.

Eventually small talk is struck, separated by times of silence as we listen and watch. Two souls wrapped in human flesh ready to take human life at a moment's notice. The thought of taking another person's life starts coming to the forefront of my conscience which startles my heart. "God: can I do this?" I ask myself, fully knowing the chances of not taking a life during my tour are slim.

Thoughts of a warm dry bed back home and snacks & real food within the house start playing havoc in my mind. I must push these thoughts out in order to maintain my responsibilities as a guard in war. I am cold, wet and hungry with still another hour to pull. Then what? I do not know. I haven't even been with my Unit a full day. I find comfort in the fact that my family, relatives, friends and church back home are praying for me. In this comfort, in the middle of this dismal situation, I am recalling to mind and heart God's advice to Joshua as he stood ready to take Moses' place, *"Have I not commanded you? Be strong and of good courage; do not be afraid, nor be dismayed, for the Lord your God is with you wherever you go."*[22]

That advice steadies my nerves, calms my heart and fortifies my mind for the remaining hour. Before I know it my shift is finished. My replacement greets me and asks how things are going. We talk quietly for a few minutes before I dismount the Track to make my way back to the bunker.

It is good to get out of the rain and my drenched flimsy poncho. I unzip my flak jacket and lay it against the small stand.

I place my helmet, ammo and canteen on the stand's top. I place my Bible and knife under my pillow. Next, I take off my saturated jungle boots, but leave my damp socks and pants and field jacket on. No one previously told me to keep dry socks and fatigues within reach. From now on I will.

At least it is dry in here - damp but dry. I eventually take off my socks as I unfold my poncho liner, slipping under it to warm myself and hopefully get some sleep. But, too many thoughts and questions fight against sleep's advancements as I lay here shivering from the cold and loneliness. I am in a bunker with other guys, but still alone in that I know none of them, nor they me.

I unzip my field jacket but leave it on as I try getting comfortable on my rickety cot. Looking into the darkness and listening to the other guys breathing, moaning and coughing, I finally surrender to sleep.

My world is rocking as I am shook awake by my Squad Leader saying, "It's time to get up. We let you sleep longer since you just got here yesterday."

"What?"

"Get up, the sun's up?"

"Huh?"

"Get out of bed now and go eat breakfast. We got a full day planned for you before we escort Engineers into the boonies tomorrow morning."

Groaning and stretching I look at my wristwatch only to groan more, seeing that I slept just three hours. I do not know it now, but most of my nights will be two to three hours of sleep - four at the most.

My jungle pants are dry, but I need to slip on dry socks and a dry pair of boots. While putting on my flak jacket I am told I will not need it, nor my helmet. All I needed is my poncho and boonie hat.

After eating my C-rations breakfast I learn what the rest of the day will entail. I will be given a crash course on driving the Duster and all the responsibilities that go with being a driver.

Yes – I got this made I think to myself, only a few hours away from having my first day with my Unit under my belt. I will be proven wrong – dead wrong."

Chapter 4

DASHED HOPES

Hope is a powerful thing in the lives of broken people in a broken world.[23] I heard many sermons in church on hope, and even more lessons on it in youth groups and summer camps before coming to Vietnam. I, like many other young men serving in Vietnam, hope out rightly (or secretly within) that 1 Corinthians 13:13 will hold true in our lives, *"And now abide faith, hope, love, these three; but the greatest of these is love."*

For some, faith is shattered. For others, hope is dashed. And for practically all, love is put to the test.[24] But, I learn quickly to tuck away love securely in the inner chambers of my heart for fear of losing it – what a mistake. It will take decades to finally deal with this mistake.

After eating my breakfast of C-rations I walk confidently around the Duster rubbing my hand on it. There is something about this deadly war machine. It looks unlike any other.

As I walk around it a second time I think of friends back home who have cars, and who I have seen walk around their vehicles rubbing them with their hands. *I do not have a car back home, but do I have a vehicle here*, I think to myself.

I cannot wait to get into the driver's hatch and get acquainted with all the controls I'll need to master. I am used to driving a M60 Battle Tank weighing 52 tons, while this thing is less than half that. The M60's driver's compartment is spacious compared to this small area. The M60's driver's hatch is dead center while the Duster's driver's hatch is dead left and the Commander's hatch is dead right.

It will take some getting used to, but I can handle it. I have confidence that this is a done deal. Later this day I'll be the driver, thus not up in the tub.

Troops are drawn to Dusters like ants to picnics, but not for the same reasons. Guys are drawn to Dusters because they are so unique and deadly. Americans and Allies love them, while our enemy loathes them.

Time is ticking by slowly this morning as I anxiously wait to show off my driving skills. I know absolutely nothing about Dusters. However, I convince myself that all tracked vehicles drive alike. All I need to do is get in the driver's seat and drive from point A to point B on the makeshift test course. *No big deal*, I think to myself - seeing the course is level with only a few twists and turns.

The morning is giving way to noon and the rain is letting up leaving massive puddles on the course. This doesn't bother me as I have driven M60 Tanks through much worse terrain. In fact, I am rather calm considering this is only the second day with my Unit of Charley Battery of the 4th Battalion of the 60th Artillery (ADA – Air Defense Artillery). Our weapons are not used against aircraft but against humans.

Waiting for my Squad Leader's arrival gives me more time to think. Too much thinking is not always a good thing. I start pondering on what anti-aircraft projectiles could do to humans. This stops me mid-step on my circular pacing between the bunker and Duster. "God, please let me be a driver," pops out of my mouth up from the depth of my soul. This in turn gets me wondering what it will be like driving this thing farther out into the boonies. After taking a deep breath or two I continue my pacing - praying the whole while.

The rain is stopping, but the humidity is 100%. A hazy vapor rises from the ground on our compound while gloomy clouds hang over the lush green mountains in the distance. I keep walking while taking everything in that surrounds me. I am wet but hopeful.

Standing by the bunker I notice guys gathering around our Duster by the perimeter. "It's time," I say to myself. My mind and heart are racing as I prepare myself mentally for the task at hand.

There's a loud pop followed by a roar as our Squad Leader backs up the Duster and drives it to the makeshift driving test course. There are four guys on board, and around four walking behind it, hoping to catch a ride when it stops. A Duster has a ride all its own, which I will soon find out.

There's a skip in my stride and a smile on my face as I approach what is to be my "war chariot" for the next twelve months. By the time I arrive there are four guys in the tub / turret with additional guys sitting on the fenders, and others standing on the heavy steel grates over the engine.

The Squad Leader exits the Track and tells me to get into the driver's seat. He points out the course which to me looks like it'll only take a couple minutes to complete. "This should be old hat for you Scholten, just remember this is a Track not a Tank," he says to me, while pointing out some differences between an M60 and a Duster. He takes me through it a second time. Then he climbs up into the tub, to sit in the gunner's seat right above and behind the driver's seat.

Here I am in the driver's seat in this steel beast on my second day with Charley Battery. I have waited for this moment all morning. I have prayed and prayed again throughout last night and this morning. "God has gotten me this far. He will get me the rest of the way," I confidently say to myself while waiting for the command to start driving.

Adjusting the seat as well as my thoughts for the coming test drive I whisper a prayer. The space is tight in which I sit, but the view in front of me is wide open within the wire, and explodes in lush greens beyond. Sitting here, I lose myself in thought of how some place that looks so beautiful beyond the wire could be so deadly.

My thoughts are interrupted by the Squad Leader's booming voice instructing me to move out. I pop it in gear and hit the accelerator jerking the Duster into action. I give it everything – conquering the course in record speed, never missing any twists or turns and plowing through deep mud puddles.

Coming to a stop I place the gear in park and take my hands off the steering T-handles, relaxing my body while preparing for the "well done" from my Squad Leader. Sitting here like a male peacock strutting its feathers I congratulate myself for mastering the course.

Within seconds my confidence is shattered like a glass cup dropped from a table, and my hope is dashed to pieces like a broken plate laying in a ruined heap.

I am shaken to the core in disbelief as the Squad Leader jumps off the Track landing in front of me. His face and neck are fire red while his knuckles are white and his hands are shaking. He does not mince words in telling me what he thinks of me.

"You idiot - you nearly killed some of those guys up top. One thing you aren't is a driver. Get out of that seat."

He turns and kicks the ground as he walks off. He is mad and disgusted while I am shocked and ashamed.

I drove that Duster as if it was an M60 Tank rather than an open tub self-propelled artillery piece. A big mistake on my part. I thought I knew what I was doing, but actually forgot one important fact – the Squad Leader's instructions. What he says goes. He commands the Track, not me. I will not repeat this mistake again.

The guys are climbing and jumping off the Track as I lift myself up and out of the driver's hatch. They had an unforgettable ride that I wish never happened. But it did, and I have to face up to it.

Swallowing my pride and clearing my throat I apologize to the guys, some of whom had never ridden on a Duster before. I also ask God's forgiveness for acting so foolishly.

I am devastated. My stomach is churning with fear of what is coming next as I recall to mind a lesson God taught me a couple months earlier in Fort Hood, Texas. It was there that I lost control of my tank without brakes on maneuvers in the steep hills of the Fort.

When the M60 Battle Tank finally came to a safe stop, everyone dismounted it - leaving me alone in the driver's compartment. After regaining my composure I prayed, "What happened Lord? I was in control."

At that very moment God spoke to my heart saying, "Robert, when you are in control you are out of control, and when you are out of control you will take people with you."

I did not know what that meant then, but I sure do now on this second day with my Unit in Vietnam. I shake my head in disbelief of forgetting such a lesson so soon, in such a place, so early in my one year tour. I walk to the bunker kicking the ground and shuffling my feet.

Entering the bunker I shuffle across the floor listening to the dirt and sand crunch under my feet, and smell all the odors ensnared in this musty place. My heart is heavy and my smile is gone as I flop myself on the bunk that wobbles under a sudden blow. A sudden blow is how I feel in this place, as I slouch on the edge of the bunk looking down at my dirty boots. The longer I linger here the more entangled I become in a web of self-pity, anger, doubts and fears.

All this is happening in my second day on this small compound which forces me to take stock of myself. Which way do I go? Submit to self-pity, or get up and start over learning from my mistakes - hoping not to repeat them. Choosing to start over, I scoot closer to the small table in order to pick up my Bible for comfort and words of encouragement.

"Hey, Cherry. Sarge wants to see you. He's up at the command post," shatters the silence.

Looking up I see someone in the doorway nodding for me to follow him. Placing the Bible on the bed I get up with a prayer to face what is coming my way. I put on my helmet and follow him.

As we walk together he says to me, "You blew it and really ticked Sarge off. But give him some slack. He's only got a few days left before going home. You scared him more than anything else."

Moments later I receive the worst news of my young life. I will be up top in the tub as a gunner in training. On this second day I have my security blanket of being a driver pulled out from under me by my own doing. It is a day never to be forgotten.

My hope of being a driver is gone, but hope itself remains. This is the beauty of hope that is often forgotten in the midst of what seems to be hopeless situations.[25] My faith is shaken, but not shattered, nor defeated. I made a mess of things, but life goes on.

I apologize to my Squad Leader who in turn says, "I hope you make it." He turns and walks away saying nothing else.

He leaves for a basecamp the next day on his long awaited journey home. His tour is done - mine is only beginning.

Once again I am pacing between the bunker and the Duster. The clouds that earlier hung over the mountains have descended upon us bringing rain with them. Soon I'll be repeating last night's guard duty routine. I am hoping to get some sleep and praying that Charlie doesn't attack. Then it strikes me, tomorrow morning our Section is to escort Combat Engineers farther out into the boonies.

With less than two days under my belt, the reality of Vietnam hits me but does not defeat me. Hope, like an anchor,[26] keeps me from drifting off into hopelessness.

Like it or not, tomorrow is coming – I hope.

Chapter 5

MOUNTING UP

Life is filled with tomorrows. Some however are cut short. Life is a lot simpler when lived one day at a time.[27] My one day at a time living in Vietnam, for less than a week, is filled with troubles. Thinking about tomorrow's escorting Combat Engineers farther out into the boonies, I cannot help wonder what it will be like.

I walk around meditating on Scriptures pertaining to living one day at a time and not worrying about tomorrow.[28] Making my way to the bunker I find a pile of sandbags. Sitting on them I pull out my small pocket size New Testament to read Matthew 6:34, "*Therefore do not worry about tomorrow, for tomorrow will worry about its own things. Sufficient for the day is its own trouble.*" Realizing the full meaning of this verse I say to myself, "Isn't that the truth?"

"Hey, what're you doing there?" one of my crew members asks me.

"Reading," I reply.

"Reading what?"

Looking up at him I say, "The Bible."

"Ya, I got one of them somewhere."

He walks toward the bunker, but before entering it he turns around to look at me. Scratching his head, then rubbing his chin he says, "Hey Preacher, you must be in good terms with the Big

Guy upstairs … Give em' a good word for me." He turns and enters the bunker to get ready for tomorrow.

"Preacher. I am no preacher," I say to myself and to God. Sitting here on this heap of sandbags I am nicknamed "Preacher." I don't want this title. My name is Bob.

The nickname sticks. Once christened with a nickname in Vietnam (or any war) you are forever known as such. Our Squad and Section all go by nicknames. These names are ours to the day we die.

Entering the bunker I hear a booming voice say, "The Preacher's here – no more cursing." This is followed by laughter and introduction of names. Shortly thereafter the guys get back into their routines of preparing for tonight and tomorrow. This is followed by some guys' playing card games.

Night comes all too quickly, and with it two shifts of guard duty, little sleep and uncertainties of incoming or ground attacks. Inside the bunker there are sounds of restless sleepers and creaking bunks. Outside the bunker there are sounds of nighttime Vietnam. Inside my heart and mind are Scriptures and thoughts of family and home. Inside all of our adrenaline filled bodies are hopes of a quiet night.

"Preacher … hey Preacher, time to get out of the sack."

"What? I already pulled my two shifts of guard duty," I mumble in the darkness.

"Get out of bed. We are mounting up soon."

Swinging my body out of the cot I stand up to stretch and gather up my gear. I put on my field jacket. Then I put on my utility belt with a canteen of water, medical kit, ammo pouch and knife. I zip up my 10 pound flak jacket, and put on my helmet. Next I pick up my bandoleer of M16 ammo clips, swinging it over my head and shoulder. Last of all I pick up my M16 rifle.

My God, I think to myself, *this is real … God help me, this is really happening.* Less than three days with my Unit I am "mounting up" on this 25 ton war chariot that is armed to the teeth and ready to slaughter anything that gets in its way.

The Duster has nearly 500 rounds of high explosive anti-aircraft projectiles tucked away in every nook and cranny outside and inside. Add to this all the ammo cans of M60 machinegun rounds and our personal weapons and ammo.

Arriving at the Duster, my Section Chief takes me aside to inform me I will be a loader. He also tells me that if we are ambushed he will take my place, while I assist the driver in pulling out ammo cans to get the rounds up into the turret. "Got it?" he says to me.

Standing here in the middle of my crew I nod my head saying, "yes." In my heart I am saying, "God help me do what I need to do."[29]

Climbing aboard I sit in the loader's seat and secure my M16. The gunner slips into his seat directly in front of me. The other two men step into the mount/turret and take their positions. The driver and Section Chief are up front in their compartments. We are all exposed to the elements and, if it happens, to enemy fire.

Sitting here, I miss my M60 Battle Tank. That was then - this is now. My thoughts are interrupted by a loud pop and roar as our Track backs up from the perimeter to meet up with our sister Track.

The engine right behind us is loud. The sound of the tracks going through the sprockets are clicking as we slowly move through the compound towards the gate. As the cold damp air strikes our faces, I wonder what it will be like when we are on the other side of the gate.

We meet up with our sister Track as we always travel in pairs.' All crews have their own personalities as do their Sections. Our Section is 220 and our Tracks are 221 and 222. 222 is nicknamed "Triple Deuce."

The darkness of night is giving way to the early rays of dawn as we go through the gate on our way to meet-up with the Engineers. It's eerie out here as I look into the retreating shadows of night, and the rising mists from the ground, and the greyish clouds suspended over the mountains.

Reality hits me when the other loader stands up to "lock & load" the M60 machinegun that is mounted next to him. This is followed by the gunner pushing the clips of 40mm rounds / projectiles down into the cannons' breeches. The other crew members lock and load their rifles, securing them within our small tight turret (officially called a "mount").

We move slowly until we hit the main road. Speeding up the wind caresses our faces and whistles in our ears as we cut through it in our open turret Track. The engine behind us is roaring. The tracks beneath us are clicking as they go through the sprockets and clattering as they pass over the road. This Duster has a ride all its own.

Looking around I see these guys watching me as I watch them watching me. I am wondering what they are thinking. I am wondering what my loved ones back home are thinking. I am wondering how my friends back in Fort Hood in their M60 Tanks are doing.

"Snap out of it Scholten," I say to myself knowing full well that I must stay focused up here in the turret. Everything is wide open from up here. There is a 360 radius view of the terrain, which means our enemy has a perfect view of us as well. I am unprotected from the elements and feel totally vulnerable to the enemy - which I have not encountered yet.

Vulnerable! For the first time in my young life I feel vulnerable 24 hours a day, and this is just my first venture beyond the gate into Charlie's territory. Scanning the terrain from up in the Duster's mount I am wondering if I'll ever get used to death's constant presence.

I have faced death before. My life was nearly taken from me as an infant in a boating accident, and again two years later due to illness. I watched loved ones die of illnesses.

But this is totally different. Accidents and illnesses aren't enemies of my life here in Vietnam – people are. A people who all dress alike and look alike to me. A people who can be friendly and deadly at the same time. Farmer by day – Viet Cong by night.

We are alone on this road as we travel northward to connect with the Engineers. Our sister Track is behind us and open road ahead of us. I feel rushing air filled with strange aromas. I see tropical trees on my right and checkered rice paddies on my left with mountains beyond. In front of me the road stretches northward as far as I can see. It stretches into a strange horizon filled with unbelievable colors. I have never seen so many shades of green. I am lost in the beauty and awe of Vietnam.

This moment of amazement is shattered with the loud noise of tracks clanging on the road next to us, and the roar of our sister Track's engine as it passes us on the left. Its crew waves, shouts and salutes as they speed by us to take the lead. My left eardrum nearly bursts from the noise. Looking to my right I yell to the other loader "Man, these things are awful loud." He in turn cups his hands in front of his mouth and yells back, "You haven't heard anything yet … wait till the forties cut loose."

I forgot about them while being caught up in the ride of my life in this deadly fighting machine. It can spit out 240 rounds of 40mm high explosive antiaircraft projectiles against humans. Sitting in this cramped space with three other men I am wondering if this forgetfulness is intentional or unintentional? My God, I'm in Vietnam. I am sure this has been said by millions: "My God I am in …" I had two uncles gassed in WWI, and my father and some uncles fought in WWII.

It's starting to rain, which feels like little needles piercing our faces. I lift my shoulders as high as they can go, and lower my head into them trying to dodge this beating. I doesn't work. I am getting drenched and begin shivering.

As we start slowing down I lift my head to see what's happening. A few hundred yards ahead, and to the right, is a short column of trucks filled with Engineers and their equipment. They are very happy to see us. Our two Tracks stop in back of them. Chief climbs up and out of his commanders' hatch, and walks over to talk to their Officer. Shortly thereafter he returns and says, "They are expecting trouble, that's why they called for Duster escort." That's all I need to hear!

This afternoon is day three with my Unit. It is also day one with my crew on escort duty into possible hostilities. I am not trained for this. I am learning by the seat of my pants, which I hope I "don't load!"

There is a strange sense of thrill, reservation and camaraderie filling the crew members - including myself. Our Track slowly pulls ahead of the convoy to take point as "Triple Deuce" pulls up the rear. Our engine roars and the tracks click while my heart does both in my body snuggled within a tightly fitting flak jacket.

Our escorting intensifies upon leaving the main road to go through small villages and surrounding countryside. The villages are filled with thatched roofed huts, narrow muddy roads and villagers walking and standing everywhere. We pass slowly through them. Our M60 machine gun is pointed to the right, and our twin 40s are pointed straight ahead and sometimes to the left. All of us are vigilantly scanning everything and everyone for possible trouble. Our sister Track is doing the same. The Engineers in between us are hoping and praying Charlie fears our Dusters.

We finally arrive at the worksite which is a large culvert bridge complex. Our Track pulls ahead to take up a defensive position above the site, while "Triple Deuce" takes a fighting position below them. Now we watch. Taking mental note of the close and distant terrain, we continually watch and listen for anything or anyone out of place. We do this the whole day.

Towards the end of the day we take the Engineers back through the maze of villages and countryside to their basecamp. We then travel on to our small firebase to take up perimeter duty during the night, and come back to escort the engineers tomorrow. Day three comes to a close.

Chapter 6

REPEAT

Arriving at our firebase the driver stops near our bunker allowing us to dismount, after which he drives on to refuel the Duster with gasoline. We do not have to rearm the Track since we didn't use any of our 40mm ammo. However, we have to clean our individual weapons as they are filthy from being exposed to the elements all day. We take care of our Track and weapons before our personal needs of cleaning up, eating and resting. This daily routine will repeat itself for my entire tour. Duster and weapons first. Crew members before self. And protect all those put in our care at all costs – up to and including our lives.

When the Duster returns to the perimeter we gather together behind it to eat our dinner of C-rations. The guys learn quickly that I don't smoke, so they swap chewing gum from their rations for cigarettes from mine. Small talk starts up as we swap various individual C-ration cans. This too will go on for the rest of my tour.

Sitting here behind the Duster with my fellow crew members, I think back to sitting around my family's kitchen table eating dinner together less than a week earlier. A kitchen filled with the aroma of freshly roasted meat, fresh vegetables, salad, homemade rolls smeared with butter and homemade cake or pie. The wonderful smells would linger into the night.

Now, I am sitting on an ammo can eating out of my mess-kit with guys I hardly know. The kitchen smells are replaced by the hot engine's fumes of gas, oil and grease. There is also the distinct smells of the metal & rubber tracks caked with dirt & mud. Nevertheless, it is still dinnertime.

After eating, we wash our mess-kits and get ready to pull two two hour shifts of guard duty during the night. Our bathroom facilities are beyond crude. There is no such thing as modesty here, and even far less far out in the boonies.

I have so much to learn and get used to that my head begins spinning. In boot camp I had two months of training to become a soldier. In A.I.T. I had two months of training to become an Engineer (water purification out in the boonies). In Fort Hood I had many months of on-the-job-training to become a tank driver. But, here in Vietnam I have had less than three days of on-the-job-training to become a crew member of a Duster.

Three days. 72 hours. My God, what have I gotten myself into? In less than eight hours I and my crew will be picking up the Engineers again. In less than an hour I will be on the Duster standing guard for two hours, with another two hour shift two hours after that one. I yawn just thinking about it.

"Hey Preacher, you have first watch," my Squad Leader informs me. I was looking forward to relaxing in the bunker getting to know the guys better, and having some quiet time of prayer & meditation. This is not to be.

When in war, your time is never your own. When in war, your time can be forever changed in a manner of minutes or terminated in seconds. When in war, your enemies have one goal – your demise. Thus, you have to be alert at all times - not just for yourself, but for your Squad/crew. This alertness and constant guarding yourself is reinforced by combat experiences. Thus, by the end of your tour/deployment your life is forever changed.

I've only had a few hours of sleep since being with my Squad. I'm hoping to get some tonight, even if it is only one or two hours. Thinking about sleep makes me even sleepier, which I fight off. The thought of being caught sleeping on guard duty terrifies me. I shiver at the thought and pray for strength and alertness.

The heat from the Duster's engine has dissipated, leaving cold Army olive drab green painted steel protective grates above it. The steel is cold and hard. Cold and hard! In my short time here I have come across some very cold and hard people. I wonder what they were like before coming to Vietnam. (The same can be said of any war.) This gets me wondering about myself. Will I too become hard & cold? Will I? "Of course not," I tell myself.

Stepping off the engine grates, I step into the mount to begin my two hour watch. The night is rapidly falling upon us, which means we have precious little time to memorize everything in and beyond the wire. This is a must for survival. Once night falls Charlie is in charge. He owns it. We respond to him. (At least us Duster crews. There are American Infantry teams that set up nighttime ambushes.)

I intently scan everything in front of me - making mental note of the wire, the kill zone just beyond the wire, the elephant grass beyond the kill zone, the river beyond the elephant grass, and the wood line beyond the river. Soon the sounds will be entirely different as well. When on guard duty you cannot miss one thing about anything. Night after night. This is only my third night. I have 51 weeks remaining. Over 350 nights of this stuff. That's not counting escorting Engineers and Infantry and Artillery farther out into the boonies and guarding them there.

I snap back to attention of what I should be doing – concentrating on watching and listening, pushing everything else out of my mind. It is a starless night. They are up there in the heavens, but are blocked by the dark clouds. Stars above and war beneath and hope in-between. There is always hope,[30] even when one cannot see it – it is there just like the stars above. "Stop it," I tell myself while looking into the darkness. I am coming to learn that guard duty is a lot harder and more intense than civilians ever can imagine or understand.

There is a mist in the air. But there is something else too! I just cannot put my finger on it or wrap my mind around it. This is new to me.

There is something about tonight I cannot explain. It is a gut level feeling that I have never experienced before. I wonder if it is a premonition of what is yet to come. My skin crawls with goosebumps. Then I get a tingle down my spine. "God protect me and my crew members,"[31] I pray softly under my breath.

I ask my fellow guard how he is feeling.

"Fine, dude. Fine," he whispers back while never breaking his gaze into the darkness.

"I got this feeling," I whisper to him.

"Forget it. It don't mean nothing.' You just got the jitters," he whispers back - this time looking in my direction with a smile.

An hour into our watch we hear something strange beyond the wire. The other guard grabs a flare and shoots it skyward. There is a long swooshing sound as the flare streaks upward, followed by a pop when it explodes, releasing a fireball on a parachute that floats earthward. An eerie sight follows as shadows sway in motion with the drifting flare. I frantically adjust my eyes to the swaying shadows in front of me. All too soon the light burns out. A crew member on our sister Track in a different location repeats the process.

My heart is beating faster than I am breathing while watching the darkness envelop us again with all its uncertainties. My fellow guard fires off a few rounds from the M60 machinegun. We watch the tracers streak through the darkness until they disappear into the elephant grass. Nothing stirs or fires back.

As my two hour shift comes to a close, I am handed a flare by the other guard and told to fire it. This is the first time I have actually fired one of these in Vietnam. It will not be the last. As it streaks heavenward I pray its descending light will not reveal enemy advances on our position. Then it hits me, if we can see the streaking flare before it bursts open - so can the enemy. They have a few seconds to hide themselves in the tall elephant grass just beyond our position.

My time is up for now. Two hours from now I will be back. In between time I will have to trust those on guard duty, as I have been trusted these past two hours. All of our lives are in their hands.

As my replacements approach the Duster I wait until he actually mounts the Track before I discontinue my gazing into the darkness. He mounts up and I dismount. He hopes the next two hours will go by quickly, while I hope they will go by slowly. Which will it be? It is not up to us.

I leave my post in good hands. I enter the bunker to flop myself into my cot for a good two hours of sleep. However, sleep comes slowly. I cannot dismiss this restless feeling I have.

Laying on my back I look upward into the darkness of the bunker listening to all the noises within it. I try shutting down my overly active mind, but as soon as I push one thought out another takes its place. It's like a never ending commercial of things I don't need or want.

The only way I know how to combat this is by prayer and meditating on the Scriptures. Now, a battle is taking place in my mind between prayerfully meditating on the Scriptures and the reality of what awaits me at all times – war. I've got to put my trust in the guards on the perimeter and the Master Guard of my life.[32]

"Scholten, it's time," the guard I am to replace tells me on his way to two hours of sleep.

Closing my eyes, I suddenly jump out of bed not knowing how much time has passed since being nudged and told of my guard duty. I grab my flak jacket and helmet, canteen, and rifle, stumbling out the door into the darkness. My heart is racing and my feet are trying to keep up without tripping and falling.

Reaching the Duster I fully expect a chewing out, but receive a greeting instead by a grateful crew member ready for a fellow guard. My concern was over nothing. I did not fall fast asleep. Weariness does strange things to weary people. Weary I am, and this is only the beginning of my fourth day. I wonder how long I can go before collapsing in exhaustion.

Once again there is a mist in the air. But, there is something else too! I just cannot put my finger on it or wrap my mind around it. My two hour guard duty is a repeat of the earlier one. Thankfully, nothing erupted in or beyond the wire.

After being relieved, I walk back to the bunker looking forward to sleep which surely will come. I collapse into the cot, flak jacket and all, falling fast asleep.

I'm having a dream that shatters my sleep with nightmarish sounds and sights and feelings. I toss & turn, but cannot shake it.

"Incoming!" We all jump out of bed and run out of the bunker's security into night's insecurity, to climb up into the Duster's mount to return fire. I cannot believe this is happening. Three mortar rounds explode on the other side of the firebase.

Off to our left, high up in the mountains, we see three more flashes. From here they resemble three flicks from a flashlight, but when the mortar rounds pass over us exploding beyond our bunker they dispel that quaint picture.

After the Squad Leader gives the target's range he yells, "Fire for effect!" The gunner fires off one round from the left cannon. The Duster jolts slightly at the discharge as we watch the tracer streak through the night, exploding in the far distance. "Fire!" is the next command.

I am as tense as a clothesline after a rainstorm. There is no time for anything, as I push absolutely every thought and feeling out of my life in order to take a life. As a loader, I am to feed this rapid firing beast 4 round clips of 40mm antiaircraft projectiles that rip humans asunder. If I miss-feed the breech it will jam, or the round will possibly explode severely wounding or killing crew members.

I have a clip in my hands ready to drop in the breech after the other loader drops his. It's my turn. The clip enters properly. I turn leftward to grab another clip. By the time I turn to the right the other loader's clip is nearly gone. I drop mine in and turn to gather up another clip.

"Cease fire!" the Squad Leader yells out over all the commotion. In the previous few seconds twenty projectiles passed through our left cannon's barrel. The barrel is steaming hot, as is the night. There is a purple haze hovering in our turret and drifting outward in the wind. There are also distinct smells of gunpowder, sulfur and sweat.

We remain in the Duster for another hour, waiting and watching for more mortars or a ground attack. Neither come, but we still wait and watch. It is what we do. After the "all clear" is sounded we realize the time. It is time to rise and ready ourselves for another day. The night sky still hasn't yielded to the morning's sunlight.

We have to clean the left cannon's barrel and wipe it down with a rag saturated with gun-oil to "blue" it, which prevents rusting. Then we have to rearm the Duster; replenishing the ammo we used.

Little sleep. Too bad. It's time to mount up again to meet up with our sister Track.

Once again the darkness of night is giving way to the early rays of dawn, as we go through the gate on our way to meet-up with the Engineers. Like yesterday, it is eerie out here as I look into the retreating shadows of night, and the rising mists from the ground and the greyish clouds suspended over the mountains.

Reality hits me when the other loader stands up to check the M60 machinegun that is mounted next to him. This is followed by the gunner pushing the clips of 40mm rounds / projectiles down into the cannons' breeches. The other crew members lock and load their rifles, securing them within our small tight turret.

We move slowly until we hit the main road. Speeding up, the wind caresses our faces and whistles in our ears as we cut through it in our open turret Track. The engine behind us is roaring. The tracks beneath us are clicking as they go through the sprockets & clattering as they pass over the road.

We pick up the Engineers by their basecamp and escort them to their worksite. However, this time we take a different route as we never travel the same way twice. We pass through a larger village that is bustling with merchants and their wares spilling out into the narrow street. We and they are tense, but we press onward. The Vietnamese know that if they touch a Duster they sign their death warrant. We know it too.

Once again we guard the Engineers while they work. At the end of their workday we escort them back home. After which we go on to our firebase to pull another night of guard duty. Then repeat the whole process again tomorrow - hopefully minus the incoming.

Chapter 7

IT'S OFFICIAL

It is official, I am to be the gunner of this Duster. It is not my decision. It is decided for me. It is beyond my control.

I hoped to be the driver, but that didn't work out. Being a loader was nerve-wracking. Being the gunner brought it to a whole new level.

There are four of us in this small tight exposed turret officially called a mount. Two loaders who feed the cannons ammo clips. One azimuth (assistant gunner) who controls the rotation of the mount. And one gunner who controls the elevations of the cannons and fires them.

It takes a crew of five or six to fully operate this thing in a firefight. The four in the mount. The Squad Leader standing on the Duster's fender directing fire. And the driver pulling out ammo from the Duster's side storage compartments and ammo canisters from its belly. This is all taking place while being shot at or mortared or both.

It is a miracle I was never wounded or killed. Many Duster crew members were during the war. Far too many.

I take my place in the gunner's seat. Directly in front of me at eye level is a circular speed ring sight having seven rings with a crosshair in the middle - through which I aim the cannons. Also directly in front of me at knee level is an elevation crank I use to elevate or lower the cannons. Directory to my right at head and shoulder level is the left cannon's breech with a "fire selector lever" on its side. This lever allows me to select auto fire (firing both cannons together), and single fire (one cannon only), and stop fire (safety). Down in front of me at foot level is a foot pedal that fires the cannons.

On the other side of the cannons sits the azimuth controller. Behind both of us sit the loaders. The spent 40mm cartridges eject out the back bottom of the breeches and slide down steel shoots, into an opening on the underside of the Duster. When the M60 machinegun is fired the spent cartridges fly outward from the Duster. While we are in the mount we are exposed to the elements and to enemy fire. It goes with being a Duster crew member.

Loading these rapid firing cannons is one thing, but firing them is entirely different. While loading them I am too busy to see who we are firing at. I know the opposite is true for a gunner.

It will be my hands elevating or lowering the cannons. It will be my eyes sighting in on the enemy through the speed ring sight. It will be my ears hearing the commands to fire. It will be my foot depressing the foot pedal - firing the cannons. It will be my nose smelling the aftermath of the cannons firings. And it will be my mouth tasting the choking fumes from the cannons.

Combat involves all human senses. Every one of them. That which was once used to embrace, express, receive and experience love, mercy and beauty is switched around to embrace, express, receive, experience, and dish out hate, viciousness and death. War can easily replace civility with savagery. War can take a soft heart and gentle soul and turn them into stone. War can change a life for life or take that life from life.

Thinking on all these things forces me to anchor my soul in the haven of God's mercy.[33] I do not want to become hard and lifeless. I want to live and let live. But "it is official" won't let me live and let live. It is out of my hands. When told to fire I will fire. Humans will be killed and some of their remains unrecognizable.

"It is official" will change my life more than I ever dreamed possible. These changes will lay dormant deep in my soul, heart, spirit and entire being for years to come. Some will slowly rise, while others will suddenly pop up, and some never to budge. Either way, all these spiritual sores will have to be lanced for the pus of war to ooze out.

Upon leaving Vietnam I buried everything negative so deeply that I was unable to remember where I entered in or left from Vietnam. I also was unable to remember most of that which occurred between those two points. It would eventually take months of professional counseling and years of care from the VA, mingled with God's amazing grace[34] & Word, to bring to light some of those events.

"It is official" came into many combatants' lives and still does today. It is official - you are a Platoon Leader. It is official - you are a Squad Leader. It is official - you are on a search & destroy mission. It is official - you are on an ambush team. It is official - you are on a suicide run. It is official - you are on a rescue flight into a hot L.Z. It is official - you are a point man. There are as many "it is officials" as there are dangers in warfare.

It has been said that war is hell. It is not. It is hellish, and far more so than most civilians can ever imagine. However, within this hellishness goodness[35] and mercy[36] do happen. How? God is present.

In the heat of battle many an unreligious person has prayed unto God. This has been happening down through the centuries.

I am a praying man from a praying family. While in Vietnam, my prayer life is honed much like a sword's edge by a master sword maker. Upon leaving Vietnam I take these disciplines and lessons with me into the future - one day at a time for decades. Prayer is not something done occasionally in life, but a way of life.[37]

Sitting in the gunner's seat, getting ready for another mission, I wonder about my position as a gunner and God in my life. In doing so I think, *my "it is official" in Vietnam is an official military order that God is sanctifying (making holy)*. Solomon in all his wisdom is right: there is a time to love and a time to hate; a time of war and a time of peace.[38] I hope and pray I make it through my time of war so I can enter a time of peace.

It is time to roll. Today is my first day as a gunner. Heading out the gate I pray I'll be able to do what I have to do when called upon to do it. It is my duty. The wellbeing of my crew and those we are escorting and protecting depends upon my obedient senses. I'm in a time of war.

Chapter 8

EXPENDABLE

It is October of 1970 in the Central Highlands of Vietnam, and there is movement everywhere where there shouldn't be any. It is night. We cannot see the enemy and they know we cannot see them. At any moment Charlie can unleash a mortar barrage, followed by a ground assault against our position. The tension in the air matches that in our bodies as we strain our eyes peering into the darkness of night. The darkness of night is nearly as dark as the darkness of war. War is bad enough, but nighttime in war is even worse.

About a half of a mile off to our right and down a steep slope there is a river with rice paddies beyond it, and mountains beyond them. Directly in front of us is the kill-zone, and a quarter mile beyond are trees and a village. To our left there is the kill-zone with flat grassy land stretching beyond for a mile or more - till it gives way to mountains.

Two of us alone in a machinegun bunker listening and watching and waiting. Our bunker is elevated about eight feet by thousands of sandbags that form a pyramid like structure. There is about five layers of sandbags on top of our wood beamed reinforced ten by six foot "lookout" with three openings – through which we look and shoot. When the enemy come they have to climb upward while we shoot downward and sideways.

Left of this bunker is our Duster - ready to unleash its cannons pointblank against them as well.

The night drags on pulling us with it. The night air is alive with the smells and sounds of tropical Vietnam. These smells drift into our guard bunker and start mingling with the odors of cigarette smoke, gun oil, moldy sandbags, damp sand & dirt, open cans of C-rations and dirty sweaty G.I.'s.

We hear something strange down by the wood-line & village so we call for assistance. From back in the safety of the compound a 105mm Howitzer fires a massive flare cluster heavenward - upon its bursting into a fireball it lights up the perimeter and beyond. In a matter of seconds night becomes day exposing everything and everyone. Whatever or whoever was there have moved on or are hiding. We know they are there. We know they know we know they are there. So they are extra careful in their tactics.

We occasionally let loose with short bursts from our M60 machinegun and shoot off an occasional 40mm grenade from our M79 grenade launcher. We watch the tracers from the M60 disappear in the trees, and the grenades explode in front of and just beyond the trees - keeping clear of the village. We also watch our wristwatches.

As heavily armed as we are - we can still be killed. Life lives on one heartbeat at a time. In war bullets fly faster than heartbeats. In war one is surrounded by war. In combat one is thrown into a feeding frenzy of weaponry upon human flesh and souls. Combat forever changes one's life.

Thinking about what could be and could happen, I shift my thoughts back to the task at hand - guard duty. If I fail, people die. If I fail, I die. This is only one watch of two watches of one night of a year's worth of nights. Night after night. It's enough to drive you mad. It's enough to get you to say, "it don't mean nothn'." "Stop it Scholten," I tell myself as I get back to the task at hand.

Our second two hour watch is more intense than the first. This time there are multiple bursts from the 105mm Howitzer, plus small flares set off by guards on the perimeter.

Watching and listening to the machinegun tracers and grenades exploding and the 105mm Howitzer firing starburst clusters, I wonder what life is like in that small village. Back home, it is quiet at night except for an occasional ambulance or firetruck siren. But here? The villagers fear the Viet Cong by day and night. And they must fear us as well – hoping our rounds do not destroy their homes, families and what little livestock and possessions they have.

The sad truth is that their meager possessions are expendable for the greater wellbeing of the big picture. What's a few chickens or pigs? It means everything if these few chickens or pigs mean their wellbeing and survival.

Decades after Vietnam people would ask if I was annoyed by crying babies in church. My response was always the same, "no I'm not bothered by their crying." They thought that as a pastor I would be disturbed by them, or that they were disturbing the congregation. I never thought about the reason behind my answer. Until! There is always until in life. Until one time someone wanted more of an answer. She got more than she bargained for … as did I.

There face to face, an inquisitive church member entered into a reluctant pastor's past to hear something she would never forget. Something snapped in my memory and blurted out my mouth before being softened by my heart. "I love hearing a child cry in church. Because, back in Vietnam after a firefight near a village during the night I would listen for babies crying. Cries told me they survived."

The woman didn't know what to say as she stood staring at me. I simply said, "Have a good day." Then I turned and walked off as if nothing happened. But, something did happen. Later that day I nearly had a meltdown thinking back to my Vietnam days. Thinking of how much was still buried deep down within wanting to come out, but was being denied.

"Have a good night?"

"What did you say?" I asked my fellow crew member who came to relieve me on guard duty.

"Was it a good night?" he asked again.

"There's plenty of movement out there, but so far so good," I reply standing up to leave the guard bunker. Yawning and stretching I shuffle back to my home away from home. So much has changed in so short a time. One thing that changed is going to church. I haven't. I haven't been to a basecamp, thus to a chapel as of yet. I wonder how long it will be before ... my mind wanders off in a different direction thinking about what's beyond the wire.

Before dawn we ready ourselves to escort a Company of 173rd Infantry Airborne out farther into the boonies. They will be riding in large deuce and half trucks to get to their entry point. We will escort them there and wait till they are out of range of our cannons. Then we will wait some more until we are radioed to head back to our compound. We will return to this point to pick up those who survive their sweep and escort them back to their basecamp.

Back from escorting the Infantry we tend to our Dusters and our individual weapons that are filthy from the elements - as are we. Equipment first and foremost, then our personal needs. Personal needs! In war personal needs are few and far between; and even fewer and farther between for Infantry personnel out in the boonies.

Today we actually have some free time. Time to write a letter or two. Time to get to know each other as much as we allow each other to know. The less the better. This is the way it is. This is the way it must be - I take it to be.

We are not looking forward to another night, knowing there will be more movement and possible hostilities. This is when free time is not a good time, because it gives you too much time to think about what could be. I rest myself and put myself at ease by reading Scripture and praying. There is so much to pray about. I find prayer comforting.

Before the night watches begin a high ranking non-com from our Battery arrives with a gift for us that will enable us to "own the night." It is a starlight scope. We couldn't wait to use it. We heard about these things, but never seen one.

But then! There is always "but thens'" in life - especially in war. The "but then" for us was when the non-con said, "Boys, you are expendable. This is not. You will protect it at all costs. It must not and will not fall into enemy hands, or there will be hell to pay."

What a statement. What a night. What a war. I am expendable in all of them. I have a soul and am made in the image of God.[39] This starlight scope is made by man for man to make it easier for man to kill man. And I am expendable! There is something wrong with this picture.

They set up the starlight scope in the guard bunker, getting it ready for tonight. I set up my personal space in my bunker to relax and have devotions and prayer. Sitting here my mind reflects upon Uriah the Hititte - a faithful general of King David.

Uriah was off fighting a war for David, leaving his wife at home. David by chance saw Uriah's wife bathing. One thing led to another, and he let his guard down. In doing so, he took her and had his way with her in a one night fling. Afterwards he sent her on her way.[40] He enjoyed himself, she didn't – but he was a king and she wasn't a queen.

That's that. At least that is what King David thought, until Uriah's violated wife sends word to David of her pregnancy.[41] Oops. Now what? David thinks fast and sends word to the battle front for Uriah to come home. He does this hoping Uriah will spend a night with his wife Bathsheba. Uriah comes back to see the King, but does not spend the night with Bathsheba. Next, he gets Uriah drunk, hoping he will go spend time with his beautiful wife - but he doesn't.[42]

Now what? Plan three! Uriah is expendable for David's sake and reputation. David arranges for Uriah to be killed in battle.[43] How many Uriahs have there been down through the centuries in wars? Too many.

A province to be taken. A city to be taken. A neighborhood to be taken. A hill to be taken. A bunker to be taken ... Only to have them abandoned afterwards. Once abandoned, the enemy slips back in them again. What about all the men's lives lost in all those "takings?" They are, it seems, expendable and easily replaceable with fresh troops.

It is hard not to become bitter when thinking about all the Uriahs lost in wars, especially those who died in your arms. I never had a fellow soldier die in my arms, but I have friends who did. I was never wounded (close many times), but I have friends who were. I never lost a limb, but I have friends who have. Their lives have never been the same because of those constant reminders.

What makes combatants rush or ride up against the enemy shooting at them, or pilots fly into flak, or sailors sail into embattlements? Orders. That's it.

In war one cannot simply walk away after having enough. One cannot give a two week notice and then go find a new job. You obey orders or pay the consequence, which could be anything from demotion of rank or imprisonment or death or all of them. There is always someone higher up in the "Chain of Command" giving orders - of whom many are nowhere near the fighting.

I am worn out thinking about King David and Uriah and what is facing me outside my new musty, damp home's threshold.

Thinking further about it, a smile comes to my face in the realization that I am known by God - even while fighting in Vietnam. Just as Uriah in his war was known by God. Uriah became a statistic to David, but not to God – thank God.[44]

The night is alive with sounds and aromas and shadowy sights as I carefully walk to the guard bunker on the perimeter. In entering the bunker I ask how the guards' night is going. Their response is not what I want to hear – a repeat of last night, with the exception of the starlight. "You got to look through this thing," one of them says to me.

I reluctantly make my way to this contraption that made my life expendable to look through it. "Wow, this is incredible. No wonder Charlie must not get a hold of it" I say in amazement. The night belongs to us now in light clear green shades revealing everything, and more importantly, everyone. Tonight we take turns looking through the scope, while the other guard mans the machinegun. We are ready to cut down anyone who the scope reveals in the darkness of night, in the darkness of a war.

Chapter 9

GUARDIAN

When in war there are a host of things one must memorize, starting with your Chain of Command. Your weapon's serial number. Your service number. Your daily and/or weekly orders. Your enemy's tactics. Your surroundings and terrain. Your fellow Squad members' locations. Your weapons location – just to name a few.

There is also something else that has been memorized by fighting men and women down through the centuries: the Twenty-Third Psalm, which reads: *"The Lord is my shepherd; I shall not want. He maketh me to lie down in green pastures: he leadeth me beside still waters. He restoreth my soul: he leadeth me in the paths of righteousness for his name's sake. Yea, though I walk through the valley of the shadow of death, I will fear no evil: for thou art with me; thy rod and thy staff they comfort me. Thou preparest a table before me in the presence of my enemies: thou anointest my head with oil; my cup runneth over. Surely goodness and mercy shall follow me all the days of my life: and I shall dwell in the house of the Lord for ever."* (KJV)

We receive orders to escort an Artillery Section of 155mm Howitzers up to a mountaintop firebase. The guys have been there before and tell me it is a treacherous trip through triple canopy, narrow dirt roads and countless ambush locations. They speak with enthusiasm, as though they can't wait to go. In fact, their faces light up talking about their previous trips and times spent at the small isolated mountaintop firebase.

I have been here with my crew for less than two months and have already seen and experienced more than I wanted. Word pictures of the journey start forming in my mind while listening to them speak. The more I listen the more colorful the pictures become. The more colorful the pictures become the more they pull me into the frame of things. Once within the frame's parameters I begin bracing up for the trip. After psyching myself up, I ready myself for an adventure.

I tell myself, "I have been shot at and mortared at, but I haven't been ambushed yet." The guys see I am deep in thought and know what I am thinking about. "You will have the time of your life Preacher - it'll be a rush. You won't even need weed or booze for the buzz you'll get," some of them laughingly tell me. They encircle me and together we walk toward the bunker to hang out.

We meet up with the Artillery in early morning for a long day's journey which is everything, plus more, of what I was told yesterday. A Duster in the front of the column and one in the back. We are in the back and are pulling a trailer with additional canisters of ammo and supplies. In the near distance we see the forested mountains drawing nearer and nearer.

I cannot believe what we are about to enter. The narrow dirt road with deep ruts is disappearing into a mountain of green trees. From here it looks like we're about to enter a tunnel.

Trees and more trees. Trees everywhere. Occasionally we break free of the triple canopy to see blue skies and a Cobra gun ship flying above us, escorting us as we escort those in our care. The Artillerymen thank God for us Dusters and we Dusters thank God for the Cobra. This gets me thinking about Psalm 23, *"The Lord is my shepherd."*[45] We are watching and protecting (shepherding) the Artillerymen as the Cobra gunship is watching and protecting us the best it can, when it can. Much of the time we can only hear the chopper, being unable to see it through the heavy canopy above us.

The guys were right! This is a rush. Any moment from behind any tree, or in any rut, or around any bend, death awaits us. This is unlike any war movie I have ever seen. Our progress is slow and tedious as we press upward to the firebase. It is afternoon and we are still snaking through this rutted tunnel of a road.

The beauty of this place is breathtaking. The journey through this place is an undertaking. The danger of this place is life-taking. The memory of this place is inescapable. All these are spinning in my head as I scan everything around and above me, while keeping myself fully alert every second of every moment of every hour. Then it hits me, once at the firebase we will have to guard the perimeter and eventually make the trip back down the mountain. This is turning into one long day. One day out of 360+ days.

Off in the distance we see our destination coming in view. From here it looks like a miniature compound assembled by a master model maker. It will be another hour or so before we reach it with our much needed convoy of artillery, ammo and Artillerymen.

We finally reach our destination near dusk. We do not know who is the happiest - the firebase personnel or our convoy. This place is truly a mountain top experience as it sits smack dab on top of a mountain. What a view! I have never seen anything like this. It is breath taking.

Our Track (221) pulls up left of a bunker on the perimeter. Our view of the surrounding mountains is spectacular. From where we are located our cannons cannot be lowered enough to hit anyone climbing up the sheer vertical mountainside. Track 222 is placed at the gate from where the crew can use their cannons against any approaching enemy.

We clean our Duster and personal weapons the best we can. This is followed by placing 40mm clips upside down on our tub's side, so that they hang ready to be picked up when necessary. We have around eight such clips, plus the four in two clip holders, plus four ammo canisters of four clips each, plus the four clips in the breeches. Eighty-eight rounds - with more ready in reserve. We dislodge the M60 machinegun and set it up in the bunker. After this we wash up using our metal pots as basins. Finally, we who are not on guard duty get to eat a wholesome supper of C-rations - which tasted mighty fine.

As dusk starts to give way to night I hear the strangest noises of my life. I ask some Special Forces what is making such racket. They tell me it is orangutans challenging us because we are in their territory. "You best let them be if you know what's best for you," one of the Green Berets tells me.

Years later, my family was visiting Brookfield Zoo outside of Chicago, wherein we entered the orangutan exhibit where a big male orangutan was quietly resting in a large fake tree. I told my little daughters that I could speak orangutan. They didn't believe me and told me to prove it. So I let loose with the call I heard so often high in Vietnam's Central highlands. The once tranquil beast swung to action within its cage, causing all of us spectators to back up in disbelief.

"What did you say to it daddy?" my youngest daughter asked me.

"I don't know? But whatever it was he didn't like it." I had long since forgotten that the only call I knew was a challenge call, which I had down pat.

As we continued our walk through the zoo I contemplated about other experiences and consequences of Vietnam. I was walking with my family, but not with them emotionally. I was in a whole different world. No! I was caught between two worlds – that of the present and that of the past in Vietnam. I thought, *should I share some of my Nam experiences with my family? Now would be a perfect time.* I chose not to. Looking back over forty years, I should have shared. I could have talked about my times up in that isolated mountaintop firebase where the nights were long and dark.

Our night here at the firebase is like being in a wild animal preserve. The night is alive with the sounds of wild animals, birds and bugs. Some of the animals can actually kill us humans.

In the morning our downward trip from this firebase is quicker than our ascent since we aren't pulling a convoy. However, we still have to be super alert the whole trip as Charlie knows we are coming down. He also knows we are vulnerable.

Vulnerability is hard to deal with in war because of its continuous presence. Being exposed to the elements for days, if not weeks, without relief wears one down. Being susceptible to bacteria, mold and mildew for months on end is disgusting. Being under continuous threat of the enemy is dreadful. Being forced to deal with life and death issues on a regular basis can harden the softest and gentlest of persons.

Later this afternoon, we meet up with another convoy of Artillery that are being escorted by another Duster Section. We join them going through a long fertile valley with mountains in the far distance. We cautiously rumble through many small villages and travel over raised narrow roadbeds between endless rice paddies. What a contrast from last night.

War is filled with such contrasts. In my case, my Section is continually on the move. Very seldom do we stay in one place for more than three weeks or so. This will eventually have a negative factor in my life.

Our two Sections' orders are to escort the Artillery to a newly developed small isolated firebase that serves as a spearhead for a chain of firebases. There is a squad of 173rd Infantry Airborne waiting for us there. Upon our arrival at the acre size base, with one strand of wire around its perimeter, we place a Duster in each of the four corners.

It is flat as a pancake with no bunkers of any kind for protection. We unload bundles of sandbags from our trailer to be filled with dirt. This is followed by unloading metal culvert halves. We place the culverts upside down and stack layers of sandbags over them. These tiny two-man dwellings, which we crawl in and out of, will be our homes for weeks to come. One of the other Sections' Duster towed a large water trailer from which we have chemically purified water. It is drinkable. We will have to use it sparingly because it is all we have. Our food is C-rations and any foodstuff we have from earlier trips to a P.X. on a larger L.Z.

Our sole purpose of being here is to protect the Artillerymen and Infantry placed in our care. Guardians of sort.

Some of us, including me, fill sandbags. Others lay out additional claymores and tripwire/flares in the razor sharp perimeter wire. Still others pull out additional ammo canisters from the Dusters. Sweat is pouring off our foreheads and down our backs and arms. All we have to clean up with is a little water in our helmets (metal pots). Tomorrow we will build ammo bunkers to protect our 40mm ammo from mortar attacks.

Night comes all too quickly, and with it the guard duties in a new location. Gone are the sounds of the Central Highlands with all its similarities. Now we are shrouded in a whole new darkness that is strangely quieter than what we are used to. It's too quiet. It's troubling. We are alone.

Tonight is a perfect time to be attacked. Everyone knows it, including Charlie. Our four Duster crews are ready to unleash devastating firepower at a second's notice. The Artillerymen and Infantrymen are relying upon us to guard them 24 hours a day - seven days a week. They feel safe with us here. We feel safe in our mounts with cannons and machineguns ready for action.

This small firebase relies upon us Dusters. We Duster crews rely upon each other's crews abilities to fight. Since our firebase is the spearhead, the others in the chain rely upon us to warn and protect them.

In war we all rely upon each other - especially during the night. We literally guard each other's backs. Thus the phrase, "I got your back" holds emotional meaning for Veterans. When we have each other's back, we are willing to give our lives for each other to keep each other safe. It is a code of conduct. It is a way of life to protect life. We are guardians. It is what we do.

There is a Guardian that never sleeps nor slumbers. There is a Guardian who has our backs. Jesus Christ the Lord is His name. He is the Good Shepherd who knows His own by name.

War haunts many of those who have been or are caught up in its madness. PTSD is such a haunting. It is real. It is all too real for all too many Veterans of all too many wars.

A first step to be taken in coming up out of PTSD's deep trench is yielding to the Lordship of Jesus.[46] I thank God for the realities of the "*Lord is my shepherd*"[47] in wartime and peacetime. He is truly a proven Guardian.[48]

Chapter 10

G.I. WANT?

While on this firebase I got my Vietnamese name of "Too Young." "Preacher," was given to me by my crew members. "Too Young," was given to me by Vietnamese children.

Each day children of all ages forge the river. Walk through the swampy bogs. And cautiously walk through our free fire kill zone up to our perimeter wire. Why? To sell us something or to receive something. Either way, they take tremendous risks in doing so. I cannot help remembering back to my childhood with all its comforts and blessings, in comparison to these poor kids. Thinking further, *I realize not many years separate me from them.* This war I am in is being fought by young people, some of whom never make it back home.

Looking at the children, through the wire, it is obvious there is a hierarchy. The wee little children who want candy & gum. The young teenagers are "coke girls" who sell cans of soda or beer. Then, the older teens who sell themselves.

These children are in a kill zone in which they are open game for target practice. They have no business in the cleared out area. Therefore, they take their lives into their own hands every time they approach the wire. Are they children or are they instruments of warfare of the Vietcong?

Many an American soldier or Marine or Sailor lost their lives, or were badly wounded, when Vietnamese children used as living bombs blew up in their midst. War is not nice. Americans do not use children as living bombs but our enemies do. And they did so with deadly results.

It is sad that so many returning soldiers from Vietnam were called "baby killers" when the opposite was more true - children were killing soldiers. By far, most American Troops went out of their way to keep children safe - sometimes to their own peril.

One early morning when the mist is still rising from the river and steamy heat vapors are rippling through the muggy air, some Vietnamese children gingerly approach our perimeter. Their smiles are infatuating, as are their sparkling eyes. Behind them are the coke girls, who are hoping to sell us some cans of beer.

The little ones are reaching through the tangled razor sharp wire hoping to receive some candy or gum. The wire could easily slice their skin wide open, but yet they persist in reaching through it. To keep them from being cut, I throw some candy over the perimeter wire to them. As they gather it up, the older coke girls come forward saying, "G.I. want beer?"

"No, I'm too young to drink beer" I reply with a smile that matches the younger children's. The coke girls smile and giggle. One of them asks me, "G.I. want to boom boom (sex)?"

I nearly fell out of my boots. I can't believe what I am hearing. I just stand here looking at her in disbelief.

Sizing me up, she says, "G.I. want mamma-son for boom boom?"

My goodness, what is next I wonder. Surely it isn't one of the five or six year old girls. Looking at her through the wire I say, "No, I'm a Christian."

To which she replies, "Christians make boom boom to make more Christians."

To which I reply, "This Christian has never made boom boom."

All the children giggle as they make a circle talking with each other and pointing at me. I can only imagine what they are saying.

Finally, I say, "I'm too young to have boom boom and to drink beer."

Once again they encircle each other chatting together in a language I don't understand. But, I know they are having sport at my expense. After a few minutes of this, one of the older girls asks me, "What is G.I.'s name?"

"My name is Bob."

"No – your name is Too Young."

As long as we are here we are visited daily by these children and sometimes mama-sons, who all call out, "Where's Too Young?" They must have many relatives, because at various isolated firebases or L.Z.'s I am called out by locals as "Too Young."

While on these small firebases we have our basic needs met by the United States Army. We have C-rations for our daily meals. We have drinkable water that smells and tastes like chemicals. We have sandbagged covered culverts for two-man shelters from the elements and mortar attacks - of which they provide little protection. But, they are better than nothing. We have helmets (metal pots) to protect our heads and act as basins to wash ourselves. We have crude toilets consisting of wood seats on top of cut-off 55 gallon metal drums. These sit in the open facing the perimeter. We have ammo for our Dusters and M60 machineguns and M16 rifles. On the down side: we have no laundry, refrigeration or electricity.

We make do with what we have. We must. There is nothing else we can do but accept our conditions and perform our duties the best we can - hoping for the best.[49] As crude as these basic items are, they are far better than some Infantry have out on patrol in the jungles & rice paddies.

There are times I think of home growing up in Chicago on the Southside, where our city blocks were larger than these little firebases in Vietnam. No need for razor sharp wire to keep enemies out of our lives. No purpose for guard duties in danger filled nights. No crude living conditions. But, just the opposite – we had it well.

One day at a time. Less than fifty of us on this small firebase in the middle of Charlie's backyard. Every night we Duster crews pull our guard shifts, resulting in two to four hours of sleep per night. Then we pull perimeter guard all day long. Eventually, we are to be relieved by fresh Duster crews.

Our release does not result in rest and relaxation. We simply go elsewhere to do the same thing. Sometimes we go to larger L.Z.'s such as L.Z. English and L.Z. Uplift - from which we pull convoy duty and guard duty.

I spend time and sweat throughout the Central Highlands and Central Coastal Lands. The only times I see major basecamps are my arrival in and departure from Vietnam.

War haunts many of those who have been or are caught up in its madness. PTSD is such a haunting. It is real. It is all too real for all too many Veterans of all too many wars.

A second step to be taken in coming up out of PTSD's deep trench is accepting the Lord's care for us, rather than pushing Him away.

I thank God for the realities of the *"I shall not want"* of Psalm 23 (KJV) in wartime and peacetime. He is truly a proven care-giver as described in 1 Peter 5:6-7, *"Therefore humble yourselves under the mighty hand of God, that He may exalt you at the proper time, casting all your cares upon Him, for He cares for you."*

Chapter 11

RELAXATION: WHAT'S THAT?

We rise before dawn again to escort Engineers out to their isolated worksite. We are heading out to a contested area. Once there we are on a large rocky hill overlooking the South China Sea. It looks like a movie poster hanging on a travel agent's wall.

Around noon Chief calls me over to where he is standing. He asks me if I want to walk with him down to a beach about two miles from our location. Since it is warm, clammy and windless; and since I'm bored to tears - I agree to join him. Walking back to the Track I retrieve my M16 and a bandolier of ammo clips for our journey.

Off we go without a worry in the world. We zig-zag down the steep hill to its bottom, where we walk on a narrow beaten down path. Chief is a giant of a man, standing well over six feet tall and weighing in over 250 pounds of muscle. Then there is me, a skinny "sad sack" five foot ten inches and weighing in at 110 pounds.

It is warm, humid and muggy as we make our way toward the beach to refresh ourselves in the ocean water and cool breeze. We are on a mission. An unsanctioned one. Nevertheless, it is an undertaking that hopefully will have a great reward. Our actions can have negative ramifications, but who cares? We are fighting off boredom and winning. The farther we venture out the greater the thrill. And the greater the thrill the grander the adventure.

When on top of the large steep hill we see only one village below. Now that we are down here, at its base, we discover there are two small hamlets. Coming upon the first one, its residents disappear into their small thatched roofed huts. Some children stick their heads out of the doorways to look at us, but are pulled back into the dwellings by their parents. Before they are yanked backward we wave to them and smile.

We keep walking on this narrow pathway that leads us to a second small village. Upon entering it, there are no people to be seen, nor even dogs. We should be taking the hint. But, we are on a mission to refresh ourselves in the sea. Besides, we are no longer bored.

Continuing our quest toward the beach a temple comes into view off in the distance. These family shrines are highly sacred to the villagers, of whom many worship their dead ancestors. We do not know how holy and special these sites are until an armed guard opens up on us. Wow, what a rush as bullets buzz inches over our heads.

Chief yells out, "Ooohhhh Scholten," as we both turn inward rather than outward. In doing so, I bounce off Chief like a rubber ball and fall backwards. He reaches out and pulls me back up as we hustle back toward the hill from which we descended. Sticking to this narrow path, we pass again through both villages whose residents are still hiding.

Upon arriving at the base of the hill, an ARVN meets us to lead us back up the steep incline. Chief starts walking up first, but the ARVN grabs hold of him telling him to stop. This is funny, since Chief is three times the size of this little fellow. But, what follows isn't funny. It is sobering. The ARVN says in broken English, "Follow me through the pineapples."

Pineapples! I do not see any pineapple plants growing on this steep rocky hill. What's this nut talking about? So I ask him, "What pineapples? There are none here."

He replies, "Pineapple field … you know landmines."

"What?" both Chief & I say in unison. We had naively walked down through a landmine field and survived. Needless to say, we walked in this guy's footsteps very carefully. Upon reaching the top, my Squad Leader chews both of us out royally, saying, "We jumped to action when those shots were fired, but couldn't see you. You could have gotten yourselves killed. What were you thinking?"

Chief says, "Leave Scholten alone - he was with me." He puts his big arm around me in a bear hug and says, "We didn't make it to the ocean, but we had a great time didn't we?" We would eventually have more such unsanctioned missions to fight off boredom.

We have another couple of hours of guarding the Engineer before escorting them back to their basecamp. Once we successfully deliver them there, we travel on to our encampment to pull perimeter guard all night. Then, come morning we will return to this same rocky hill - minus the side agenda of walking to the beach. It will be hard looking out over the panorama without venturing down into its beauty. But, we learned our lesson - somewhat.

I should have been killed many times over. Boredom is a killer to fight, but it has to be fought off in order to keep alert. Why? Because at any second, on any day, Charlie can launch a mortar attack or something worse.

Once caught up in armed conflict adrenaline kicks in. Then, everything kind, wholesome and lovely are pushed out of our hearts and replaced with a single-mindedness of "to kill or to be killed." Afterwards we tremble in our boots. My hands shake uncontrollably until I calm down. Taking human lives is not natural, but in war it becomes a norm – a terrible norm at that.

Looking back to that fateful day, I laugh and wish I could sit down with Chief to recount that shared adventure. We had many such exploits. What made us do them? Boredom – we needed adrenaline rushes. After all, we would only be here once – Lord willing.

Chief and I, along with some other crew members from our Section 220, had many side adventures together. It was a miracle we all survived. We pushed fate for fate's sake to live on the edge between life and death. A lot happens in war besides war. There are many ways to die in war.

Whenever we have down times of a few days we eventually get itchy to get back out where the action is. Why? For the thrill of it all as we face death and survive. Like it or not, "It don't mean nothin'" is starting to take hold.

In my first month in Nam, if guys had told me I would do anything to get out of the security of a large L.Z. to get back into the thick of things - I would have told them they were crazy. But, something happened. My crew became my family. Where my family was is where I wanted to be. And the purpose of my family became my purpose – live to fight. In the midst of it all, I did my best to keep myself and fellow Section members bathed in prayer, and comforted myself with the Bible.[50]

After this full adventurous day, we still have to pull perimeter guard duty all night. I have the second watch, which means I have time to relax. Laying face down on my bunk in the dingy bunker, I turn on my flashlight and open my Bible. I savor this time of holding the Scriptures in my hands, and smelling the leather cover that binds the pages within. I rub the cover with my fingers. Then I open it, flipping the pages to Psalm 23 where I meditate upon *"He maketh me to lie down in green pastures …"*[51]

The purpose of making His sheep lie down is to rest them for their own good, or they would just wander off eating themselves to death, or get themselves eaten by wild animals. Thinking on this, I realize that today I was a wayward sheep that refused to rest, and almost lost my life multiple times.

Boredom drives me nuts. Something strange happened in my life that changed my life for the rest of my life after Vietnam. I associated rest and relaxation with boredom, so I fought them off with every fiber of my life. That opened a door to isolation in the midst of family and friends. I am not alone, am I?

After being shot at, mortared, surviving countless firefights, and staring death in the face, civilian life is flat out boring. This is something I fight off daily as I know life is worth the living, especially a life redeemed by the Lord who cares more for me than I do for myself.

Forty-five years after Vietnam I am still learning what it means to rest. My family and friends for decades have told me I don't know how to relax. They are right. It is time I try to inform them why. It is time to do something about it. It is time to yield. It is time to take deep breaths and relax. It is time to rest in the Lord.

War haunts many of those who have been or are caught up in its madness. PTSD is such a haunting. It is real. It is all too real for all too many Veterans of all too many wars.

A third step to be taken in coming up out of PTSD's deep trench is resting in the Lord, who has our best interest in mind.

I thank God for the realities of the "*He maketh me to lie down in green pastures*" of Psalm 23[52] in wartime and peacetime. He is truly a proven respite as described in Psalm 37:7-8, "*Rest in the Lord, and wait patiently for Him; do not fret because of the man who prospers in his way, because of the man who brings wicked schemes to pass. Cease from anger, and forsake wrath; do not fret – it only causes harm.*"

Chapter 12

WATER

Growing up in the city of Chicago, we had fabulous tasting water which was purified in Lake Michigan's various purifying plants in the lake itself. It still has the best water of major cities, especially when it is chilled.

What a contrast I ended up with in Vietnam. Over forty years later I can still smell and taste Vietnam's lousy water in my mind. I can also still smell my sweaty dank green poncho and damp filthy jungle fatigues.

If I could have it my way, I would have fresh clean sheets every night. I never wear socks for more than one day, and if they get damp or wet I change them. If my underwear and T-shirt get damp from perspiration I change them - if I can. I hate walking around in wet clothes. Why? Because in Vietnam there were times I remained damp or dripping wet for days on end. To this day, a whiff of mildew or mold activates fresh memories of Vietnam that can ruin my day - if I let them.

One of the small firebases our Duster guarded in November of 1970 was in the middle of nowhere, surrounded by a lot of nowhere. All we had for water was one water tank and a few water containers on our Tracks. However, within a quarter mile walk there was a slow flowing muddy river. Once a week each Duster crew got a chance to walk to the river to bathe. Each crew took the walk armed to the teeth. We all carried our M16's and bandoleers of ammo clips, except me - I carried the M79 grenade launcher and a bandoleer of grenades. Upon reaching the river, three of us would bathe while two others would stand guard: one for snakes and the other for Viet Cong. When the three of us were finished bathing, we would stand guard while the other two bathed in the muddy water. Lord knows what parasites we picked up.

Once arriving in Vietnam I never saw a bathtub until arriving back in America. Some of the larger L.Z.'s we were on had makeshift showers, of which some only contained cold water. Those cold showers felt good on steamy hot days, but were bone-chilling on cold nights in the Central Highlands during the monsoon season.

I remember one time, after coming back from an all-day escorting of a Company of 173rd Infantry Airborne, I was chilled to the bone and dead tired. It was a long day of eating dust and running into scattered downpours of rain. It was one miserable day.

The L.Z. we were located on had a large one-room hooch with mosquito-net covered bunks. It also had a wooden toilet shed with commodes and urinals. That shed also had three makeshift shower stalls and four or five sinks - all which only had cold water. Both the hooch and toilet facility were protected by layers of sandbags stacked around them, and on top of their metal roofs.

By the time we parked our Duster at the perimeter and prepared for the next day's mission it was already nighttime. Guys were jumping in and out of cold showers, or splashing themselves in the sinks, to wash off all the red dirt caked on their faces, necks and hands.

The thought of an ice cold shower didn't please me. So when told that a shower stall was open I said I had washed up in a sink. One of the guys looked at me and said, "You did not."

I argued with him as I unzipped my sleeping-bag, crawled into it, and tucked myself in. He insisted I didn't wash. I just rolled over. Finally Chief said, "Leave him alone." Good old Chief.

The next morning when I awoke and shuffled to the shower and sink area, I was shocked at what was gazing back at me in the mirror. There in the mirror, was a red dusty face with white circles around the eyes where my goggles had been while riding in the Duster. I looked like a raccoon – a lying raccoon. I stripped off my dirty clothes and jumped into the ice cold shower.

Water is vital for life. It always has been and always will be. Water is a strange thing. It can be a blessing or a curse. It can maintain life or take life. It can be fresh, salty or stagnate. It can be in the forms of liquid or steam or solid.

I heard about monsoons before going to Vietnam, but I never experienced them. Growing up in Chicago, I and many of my friends played a lot of softball - come rain or shine. While playing ball we weren't far from home. So after a game in foul weather we simply went home and changed into dry clothes. I was never wet for more than a couple of hours. During the school year we walked to and from school in sunshine or rain or snow. We had raincoats and galoshes that kept us dry going to school in the rain. During winter we had heavy coats, hats, gloves and boots to keep us warm & dry.

What a contrast during my Vietnam tour. A couple hours of being rained on turned into days on end. There was no relief from it, especially while on the Duster. Our sleeping bunkers kept the rain out, but were damp, humid and muggy within. Our tiny shelters in the boonies were clammy and cold during the monsoon season, and hot and muggy during the rest of the year. But they were far superior to what many Infantrymen had out in the jungles.

The 40mm projectiles were so sensitive that heavy rains during the monsoon could detonate them shortly after being fired. That could be dangerous. The opposite was true also. During the dry season pellets of sand bunching up off of bunkers we fired over could detonate the rounds.

War is miserable. Thank God for that. There will be wars and rumors of wars until the end of time. God help us. No one fully understands all the ramifications of war in a combatant's life during and after war, except one who has walked or ridden or flown or sailed in his or her boots.

After being joked about for a couple of days my life returns to normal as a Duster crew member. Everything together. We are a tightknit team that needs each other to function and survive. The long days and endless nights continue. The times of sheer terror, and times of total boredom, linger about us like unwanted company.

It's been one long day of being rained upon and I am looking forward to a reprieve from it tonight. Our L.Z. has a dry hooch. There is a guard bunker next to our Duster, thus we will be somewhat dry on guard duty. We'll jump into the Duster to fight if something happens. Hopefully it will be a quiet night. I can handle listening to the rain. At times it can actually be soothing, much like listening to a lullaby before drifting off to sleep.

After cleaning my weapons, and eating a meal of C-rations, I sit on my cot preparing myself for devotions and prayer. This is something I do nightly. There is so much to pray about and so much to unwind from. Sitting here: my mind, heart and soul join together in yearning for peace.

I think about peace and still waters. I open the Bible to Psalm 23 and read *"he leadeth me beside still waters."*[53] This sounds good. Sheep are afraid of running water – they think they are going to drown. If their wool gets waterlogged it will be too heavy to keep them afloat, and down they'll go. So, by *still waters* they can drink without fear of drowning.

75

I'm drowning in thoughts of home, family and friends. During the day, if we are on a mission, such thoughts are dangerous because they sidetrack our attention from tasks at hand. There is no room for such niceties when we are on a mission. We have to push them out of our minds and hearts for a spell. Hopefully, some day we will see them again.

I find *"he leadeth me beside the still waters"*[54] comforting. The Lord enables me to experience peace[55] in the midst of war, because He is the Peace that surpasses all understanding.[56] He is the Living Water[57] that saves[58] and refreshes[59] weary souls, of which I am one.

War haunts many of those who have been or are caught up in its madness. PTSD is such a haunting. It is real. It is all too real for all too many Veterans of all too many wars.

A fourth step to be taken in coming up out of PTSD's deep trench is following Jesus to the still waters of His presence, and partaking of His living water of salvation.

I thank God for the realities of the *"He leadeth me beside the still waters"* of Psalm 23[60] in wartime and peacetime.

He is truly a proven source of refreshing peace as described in Acts 3:19, *"Repent therefore and be converted, that your sins may be blotted out, so that your times of refreshing may come from the presence of the Lord."*

Chapter 13

RESTORATION

There are pictures in my mind that I wish could be erased. I wish I could click a spiritual mouse to delete experiences and dump them into a secure trashcan. I have tried many times of ridding myself of them, only to have them reappear like annoying pop-up advertisements on my computer screen.

So many pictures! Pictures in living color preserved forever in my mind that feeds my heart, that doesn't know what to do with them - so it crashes. A broken heart is hard to mend at times.

War is a seedbed of good and bad and terrifying memories. Some seeds are so horrific that the mind and heart and spirit imprison them under lock and key - never to be released. Other seeds are comical. Yes, some funny things happen in war. Then, there are the countless images in between. It is like sitting in front of a flickering television screen watching an endless review of a time wished to be forgotten.

I dream in color. My wife dreams in black & white. I remember my dreams. My wife doesn't remember hers. My dreams are graphic. My nightmares are terrifying. My flashbacks are horrifying.

I wish they all would simply go away - or do I? They are a mixture of terrible and good times woven into an emotional and spiritual tapestry. This wall-hanging is securely attached within my soul, where only I can see it through my mind's eye. There are times I catch sight of it, resulting in battles within my heart. These battles are tiresome and rob me of strength and time that should be used for wholesome living.

Since leaving Vietnam, I have only met two guys from my Section: one of my Squad Leaders and one of my Section Chiefs. They are my brothers in arms. They are my brothers I never had growing up in a family with two sisters.

I prayed for my crew members, all who I only knew by nicknames, long after leaving Vietnam. I also prayed I would eventually meet some of them. That prayer took over thirty-seven years to be answered. It was well worth the waiting. First came my third Chief of four (David = Chief). Then came one of my many Squad Leaders (Robin = Bird).

After nearly losing my life to kidney disease in April of 2014 Robin phoned me. We had an emotional few minutes together over the miles that stretched back through time to 1970-1971. Robin, a registered nurse, said he was ready to come to Kentucky from Massachusetts if I needed him. He also told me to hold on, as there were only three of us left. That was a sobering thought. (Hopefully, there are more guys to be found.) David also told me he was praying for me and my family. The band of brothers remains strong.

I never want to lose sight of what I have seen develop over the last decade of friendship with my Section, and with my fellow Duster Veterans, as we gather together at various reunions. It is at these reunions God started a healing process in my life as long lost memories began reappearing. I had completely blotted out everything negative and most combat experiences. I buried them so deep, for so long, that I lost all knowledge of them. I was dumbfounded and deeply moved various times upon hearing about shared experiences in Vietnam, long since locked up deep in my soul. These were joined by experiences brought to light through months of professional counseling and years of therapy in the VA. I am still under the care of the Lexington, Kentucky VA, of which I thank God. In fact, this book could not have been written without all of these.

In life there is good and bad.[61] There is virtue and evil.[62] There is love and hate.[63] There is kindness and there is hostility.[64] There is war and there is peace.[65]

Solomon was right when he expounded upon the various seasons and purposes in life.[66] Like it or not, stuff happens in life. It is what we do with it that makes us or breaks us.

365 days in a tour of Vietnam. We started to count them down upon landing in Vietnam. We lived for our DEROS. Nearly sixty thousand never made it to their DEROS date before being snuffed out. Then there are all those who left Nam physically maimed for life. And there are the countless thousands who left Vietnam with unseen internal wounds, which eventually surfaced as PTSD. These are not only true of Vietnam Veterans but Veterans of all wars.

To this day, there are many triggers in my life that can instantly alter my state of mind or my conduct if they are set off. They are ever present, which makes life interesting. My wife knows some of them, as do my daughters. They have seen the results of triggers being activated. These are incidents not easily forgotten. Nevertheless, my family continues to accept and love me. This is not always the case with other Veterans' families.

Some of my triggers are rain, mildew, mold, tree-lines, potholes and wet clothes. I have a host of other triggers that are activated by sight, sound, smell, taste or touch, if I let them. I left Vietnam, but Vietnam never left me. The same is true of many Veterans of many wars.

One night, in the darkness of night in the darkness of war, I was manning the M60 machinegun in a guard tower when a flare lit up the sky. To this day I can still feel the cold steel of the gun's trigger on my finger, and can still see the Viet Cong fall to the ground. It is forever etched in my mind and soul.

I can still see the Duster's crosshair ring I aimed the cannons through – it is ever present. I can still hear the cannons being fired and the rounds hitting their mark – it is ever present. I can still smell the fumes of the cannons after being fired – it is ever present. I can still feel the ride of the Duster – it is ever present. I can still see, feel, hear and taste the monsoon season – it is ever present. These and many others will be with me the rest of my life. They have become a way of life. God help me.[67] He has.

God is working on and in me, much like a master carpenter works on renovating an old house that many other people have overlooked or given up on. There is much work in such restoration that is an ongoing project. I thank God that He doesn't give up on His refurbishing project in my life.[68] He sees something in me I do not see.[69] I am of great value to Him.[70] After all, I am made in His image.[71]

I rejoice in the fact that "*he restoreth my soul*"[72] in the midst of gut wrenching experiences and haunting memories. I am just as thankful He upholds me in His Spirit[73] when I feel like collapsing under PTSD's heavy load.

War haunts many of those who have been or are caught up in its madness. PTSD is such a haunting. It is real. It is all too real for all too many Veterans of all too many wars.

A fifth step to be taken in coming up out of PTSD's deep trench is to accept the Lord's restoration attempts in our lives, rather than closing our heart's doors on Him.

I thank God for the realities of the "*he restoreth my soul* (KJV)" of Psalm 23 in wartime and peacetime.

He is truly a proven source of joy as described in Psalm 51:12, "*Restore to me the joy of Your salvation, and uphold me in Your generous Spirit.*"

Chapter 14

LEADING ME OR LEADING ME ON

There are always leaders and followers. The Military likewise is made up of leaders and followers. It always has and always will have such a structure. I was a follower in the Military.

In Vietnam, when Dusters pulled convoys there were always lead Tracks that led the way, and Tracks bringing up the rear. Sometimes there were additional Dusters or Quad-Fifty Gun Trucks.

Being lead Track is nerve racking at times, nevertheless we usually hope for that position. Why? For the rush. War does strange things to you. Stranger still is what war does to you after you leave it for home. For some combatants, war hitches a ride home with us and hijacks our families.

In the Infantry, the lead Troop on a patrol is called point or point-man. This is one of the most dangerous positions to fill. The point-man has to be constantly alert for dangers such as booby-traps, snipers, ambushes and enemy soldiers. Thus, point-men have to hone in all their senses, while walking gingerly one step at a time, knowing the next step could be their last.

For as long as there has been Infantry there have been point-men. You just do not leave such a thing on the battlefield upon your DEROS - you bring it home with you. There are all too many Veterans still walking point through emotional and spiritual battlefields. Some of these battles are of our own making, while others are not.

The leaders of Duster Sections were called Chiefs. The leaders of each Duster were called Squad Leaders. The remaining crew members were followers. We followed the commands of our Squad Leaders, who followed the commands of our Section Chiefs, who followed the commands of our Battery Commanders, who followed the commands of our Battalion Commanders. There were always commands to follow. Some were harder than others. Some made sense, while others made no sense at all. Thus the nature of war.

While out in the boonies we seldom saw Officers. Our Sections were run by noncoms – Sergeants. We rather enjoyed that. We didn't have to worry about "spit and shine" which would have been next to impossible, given our locations and responsibilities. Our Chiefs took good care of us. They had to. Our lives depended upon each other's ability to perform our duties twenty-four hours a day.

I seldom saw Chaplains or had the privilege to attend chapel. The only times I saw a Chaplain was when we were on large L.Z.'s for a period of time. All together I remember attending chapel services less than five times during my tour of Nam. Our Battalion had a Chaplain. But our Battery (Charlie) was so widely geographically scattered, that it was nearly impossible for the Chaplain to make personal visits to our locations. Chaplains had their work cut out dealing with broken lives, hopes and dreams of Troops under their care.

During one particular convoy detail in late 1970, our Duster 221 brakes down. The convoy has to continue, so our sister Track 222 leads them to their destination. Additional Dusters meet up with them to help escort. However, we are on our own in enemy territory.

Chief commands me and a loader to take the M60 machinegun and additional ammo up to the top of a high ridge off to our right. Off we go, lugging the gun and ammo can containing a belt of 7.62mm bullets. Being a SPC4, I was placed in charge of the M60.

We both wonder how four guys can handle the 500+ pounds sprocket. We forget we have a human crane among us. Chief surprises everybody by single-handedly removing the sprocket and later lifting it back in place.

Up on the ridge's crest, we see a patrol walking across a rice paddy dike a mile or more from our location. They are too far away for proper identification. We inform Chief of their presence and location. We do not know if they are Americans, ARVN, NVA, or VC. All we know is we do not want to find out. In a few minutes they are out of sight. It will take them some time to climb up the ridge and more time to advance our way.

We inform Chief we lost sight of them. Shortly thereafter we are called back to the Duster. We lift up the M60 and ammo can to the mounted crew members who secure the gun. The crew fixed the disabled Duster in record time. They are filthy dirty and exhausted, but they got the job done under the leadership of Chief.

We will follow Chief anywhere anytime. He is a true leader of men who looks out for his men, and takes great care of them. He is a warrior with a compassionate heart.

Our Section is traveling to pick up a convoy, when we are flagged down by some children in the middle of the road. This can be a dangerous situation. Do we run them over? Do we shoot them as possible enemy? Or do we stop to see what they want? Chief makes the call – we stop. Come to find out, one of the children's siblings' fell into an abandoned well and couldn't get out. Is it a trap? Is it a snake-pit?

Chief has Triple Deuce's crew dismount and follow him to the pit. They are "locked & loaded," ready for possible trouble.

Our Track stands ready to assist with firepower if needed. Arriving at the scene they hear the cries of a child from deep down in the pit.

First, a crew member retrieves a bilge pump from our Duster and starts pumping out water. Then they get a rope to pull the child up, but the child can't hold on to it. Eventually, one of the crew members' volunteers to be lowered down head first, while other crewmembers hold his legs. Talk about faith! He grabs the child and his fellow crew members lift them both up to safety.

This event is forever logged in my heart, never to be forgotten. Photographs I take of it preserve it for generations to come. It is important that people know acts of compassion take place in times of war. We come through it well, as does the child. I am sure other acts of compassion in time of war do not fare as well.

Our link-up with the convoy is delayed today. The convoy is still there, ready to be escorted. The war is still around us, ready to be fought. The day is still today, with hours of sunlight remaining. Our leader took charge and we followed him on a mission of mercy. There will be plenty of times for us to follow him on missions into harms' way.

Wars are fought one day at a time. These days stretch into weeks, which stretch into months. All too often these months stretch into years. God have mercy[74] when they stretch into decades.

When caught up in the madness of combat, time seems to stand still. It is we who are moving, not the clock's hands. It is we who are pouring all our energy into surviving and into killing enemies. It is we who stand on the edge of eternity, facing death in the eye. In the midst of it all, we follow our leaders.

I rejoice in the fact that "*he leadeth me;*"[75] and that He has plans for me;[76] and that I do not walk alone.[77] I am thankful that when I stumble on the paths God sets before me that He picks me up,[78] cleans me up,[79] encourages me,[80] and leads me on in His name.[81]

I thank God He does this for me during my war experiences and my long journey home from war.

War haunts many of those who have been or are caught up in its madness. PTSD is such a haunting. It is real. It is all too real for all too many Veterans of all too many wars.

A sixth step to be taken in coming up out of PTSD's deep trench is to follow the Lord's leading on the paths He places before us. Especially the straight and narrow path[82] that all too many people choose not to follow, or sidetrack from it for a spell.[83]

I thank God for the realities of the "*he leadeth me in the paths of righteousness for his name's sake*"[84] of Psalm 23 in wartime and peacetime.

He is truly a proven Commander who is willing to walk "point" for us through the hazards of life as described in Psalm 5:8 "*Lead me, O Lord, in Your righteousness because of my enemies; make Your way straight before me.*" And Matthew 6:13, "*And do not lead us into temptation, but deliver us from the evil one. For Yours is the kingdom and the power and the glory forever. Amen.*"

Chapter 15

DEATH

I am a fortunate one in that I cheated death multiple times in Vietnam. Death surrounded me, but didn't capture me. Death sought me, but didn't find me. Death wanted me, but was denied me.

Nothing prepared me for the utter brutality of death in war. Back in the 1960's, the movies and television programs were not as graphic as present day productions. Decades later people were horrified at the gory images in "Saving Private Ryan." Thank God. The viewers' were in a safe environment watching a staged action-packed war motion-picture. They didn't smell the images. They didn't hear the total deafening noises of combat. They didn't feel the sweaty, bloody mess laying in a heap on the ground. War did not touch them. They were safe. They could walk out. They could drive back home.

War caught up to me and touched me. It was terrible. I was no longer sitting in a theater seat watching an action-packed war motion-picture. I was in a Duster's gunner seat in a war.

Seeing human beings split open with their intestines spill out on the ground and their life's blood gone is unforgettable. Seeing human bodies beheaded and dragged through the dirt by ARVN's is forever etched in my mind. Seeing an unarmed Viet Cong murdered by an ARVN Officer is also unforgettable. These and other sights are mine forever. They are not faded black & white photographs in an envelope buried in a trunk in a basement or attic. They are vivid colored images in my heart.

War is not nice - it is terrible. War is not clean - it is dirty. War is not simple - it is complicated. War is not cheap - it is costly. War's negative factors are too often forgotten for too long by too many people - including leaders.

War is filled with death – brutal death. War reeks with death. The trouble with war is that it never ends on the battlefield, but is brought home with the warrior. It is just a different type of conflict.

Regarding myself, I left Vietnam, but it never left me. In fact, it eventually hijacked my family, which started a whole new battle for me. I am not alone in this. It has been going on in combatants' lives for eons.

There are many deaths in war. Shortly after I arrive in Charlie Battery, our Squad receives a new crew member who is just married before coming to Vietnam. He proudly shows us his wedding picture. His young wife is stunningly beautiful. We are happy for him. He has a hard time adjusting at first, because he can't get his bride off his mind. Like the rest of us, he has to push loved ones out at times to keep himself alive in the insanity of war.

Then it happens. A few weeks under his belt in Vietnam he receives a Dear John Letter – she is divorcing him. His world crashes, taking us his crew members with him. How can she do this to him? How can she do this to us? If thoughts can kill, she'd be dead. What can he do? He is stuck in war, with a whole new war on his hands and in his young life.

Lord only knows how many Dear John recipients simply gave up and took themselves out, one way or another. Demise of dreams and hopes for the future while fighting to survive in war is another form of death. The dark realities of war can choke life out of hopes and crush ambitions of dreams. Thus a terrible question sneaks into weary lives - what do we have to live for?

The suicide rate among Service Members and Veterans is staggeringly high and climbing. There is something wrong and needs to be addressed. Life is worth the living, regardless of the situations that engulf it. Life is precious. One of the horrors of war is the taking of precious lives by other precious lives. Kill or be killed. You do what you got to do. There are many untold ramifications to this "doing" of which civilians are clueless.

The Veterans Administration has it hands full in dealing with suicidal men and women, who have or are presently serving their Country in the Military. The V.A. is providing help through means of counseling, therapy, and in-house programs that give hope for these who are at wits-end.

Hope is a hopeful thing. It is amazing the confidence, courage and fait hope can muster up in one's life in the middle of war. It can be a driving force. It can be a secure haven. It can be an enduring confidence. It can be a light at the end of the tunnel.

True enduring hope is found in God. I made peace with God before going off to Vietnam, just as my father did before going off to WWII. It was easy for me as I was a Christian from a Christian home. But Hebrews 10:31 still lingered in the back of my mind, *"It is a fearful thing to fall into the hands of the living God."*

God is immortal.[85] I am not. I can pass from life to death in a heartbeat.

Before and during Vietnam I was ready to meet my Maker. My mother, sisters and close relatives were not ready for my meeting Him. They wanted me home with them. They counted down the days of my tour, praying themselves and me through each one. They were not alone in this. Millions of other family members were, and still are, doing the same thing. The loneliness and anxiousness of family members waiting for hope in the form of letters was indescribable. Days, sometimes weeks went by before such hopes made it to their mailboxes. Thank God for today's quick forms of communication.

My mother often said after my tour of Vietnam that no one would ever know what she went through while I was there. That statement is true of all loved ones of all men and women sent off to fight wars. That statement was my mother's last words to me on her deathbed. God have mercy, she carried Vietnam throughout her life, right up to the last days of her life this side of heaven.

My journey home from war has been a long one and is still ongoing. But I have hope, and I rejoice in this hope, knowing that its foundation is flawless and can hold me up through the rest of my journey. I thank God for my valleys, because while in their depths I learn afresh the power of God's amazing grace. Such grace lets me see what otherwise is so often missed – the wonder and beauty of life itself.

While experiencing the *"valley of the shadow of death"*[86] in Vietnam I learn an important lesson. I am not clinging to God's grace, His grace is firmly clasping me. I am still in war with all its uncertainties and terrors, but I have peace with the Prince of Peace.[87]

War haunts many of those who have been or are caught up in its madness. PTSD is such a haunting. It is real. It is all too real for all too many Veterans of all too many wars.

A seventh step to be taken in coming up out of PTSD's deep trench is to allow God's grace to have its perfect way with us in an imperfect world - knowing we can live above fears.[88]

I thank God for the realities of the *"Yea, though I walk through the valley of the shadow of death, I will fear no evil"*[89] of Psalm 23 in wartime and peacetime.

He is truly a proven Giver of good gifts as described in Romans 6:23 *"For the wages of sin is death, but the gift of God is eternal life in Christ Jesus our Lord."* And in 1 Corinthians 15:55-57, *"O death; where is your sting? O Hades, where is your victory? The sting of death is sin, and the strength of sin is the law. But thanks be to God, who has given us the victory through our Lord Jesus Christ."*

Live in that victory, my friends. Read the following carefully and receive it faithfully, *"The Lord bless you and keep you; the Lord make His face shine upon you, and be gracious to you; the Lord lift up His countenance upon you and give you peace.* (Numbers 6:24-26)."

Chapter 16

COMFORT

Our position is targeted and the incoming rounds are walking towards us. It is just a matter of time before they land right on top of us. During this exchange our left cannon's breech jams. I instantly put the safety on and yell for the crew to use the right cannon. But the loader keeps trying to free the jammed projectile which can explode - injuring or killing us. Finally, he clears it after the incoming is over. Or is it? We don't know what is next. More incoming or a ground attack? Is Charlie giving up, not wanting to face our 40mm cannon fire? It can be a different situation if they know our cannon is jammed.

Decades later I still think of that night and other such nights of uncertainties. I still hear, see, smell, feel and taste those encounters. Dreams are made up of them. Conscious hours are harassed by them. Unseen battles still rages on at times … if I let them. I am getting better at defusing the triggers that send me back to Vietnam through intrusive thoughts or flashbacks. Life goes on, but it is different. At times it is a good difference, while at other times it isn't.

I am weary from forever fighting intrusive thoughts of Vietnam. It would be wonderful to go through one day without experiencing any such thoughts. If I could get through one day, then just maybe I could get through two days. What a relief it would be in a life stained by war.

What are intrusive thoughts? Thoughts of Vietnam (or whatever war) triggered by every day experiences. That is why these thoughts are so wearisome and in some cases outright dangerous.

When I put pills in my weekly pillbox, my mind flashes back to Vietnam when I placed shells in my M16 clips. When driving in a vehicle with its windows down, the breeze takes me back to when I was riding in the open turret Duster. When I see tree lines in the distance, I am catapulted back to Vietnam, from which the enemy fired on us. Obstacles or potholes in the road are instant reminders of watching for landmines while on escort duty in Nam. When drenched by downpours, I remember the long monsoon days and nights from which there was little relief.

Roadkill is a trigger for me, especially if I cause it. For years Cheryl was clueless while traveling in the car with me of what was happening in my heart and mind. A dead animal on the side of the road was just a dead animal in her eyes. It was far more than that to me. Hitting a small pothole was just a bounce to her, but not for me. Coming upon a detour was just an inconvenience for her, but a potential ambush for me. I would become quiet or my temperament would instantly change for a matter of hours, or the rest of the day.

Presently, Cheryl is aware of these triggers and works me through them by gently reminding me of what is happening. It has been a long journey for Cheryl as well. I tremble at the thought of life without her. I thank God she has never given up on me. Her "I do" was truly "I do," as was mine. I find great comfort in the security and wonder of our marriage and family.

Music is another trigger for me, as is cold food. I ate enough cold food in Vietnam to last me a lifetime. I want my cooked food hot and my water ice cold.

Smells and unexpected noises are more triggers for me and other Veterans. They are probably the worst of all, because they come out of nowhere – they sneak up on you – just like enemy do in war.

While in Vietnam we called our home back in America the "real world" and civilians living there "normal ones." We called the airplane taking us home after our tour the "freedom bird," and the airplane taking the dead back home the "ghost ship." Most of us couldn't wait to get on the freedom bird. We counted down the days to our departure from Nam to the real world, to be among the normal ones.

Once back home many of us, if not most, stepped out of one war only to step into another with multiple fronts. The normal world was no longer normal, it was just as insane as the war we left. We were caught between two worlds, so we did what we needed to do – fought on.

This new war needed new tactics, which we quickly discovered and implemented in our lives. They worked all too well for all too long. Forgetting the past in order to survive the present takes everything from a person and gives very little back. Years turned into decades before we realized the deadly cost of this war.

I personally developed a tactic that worked wonderfully well for me. I simply stuffed all my combat and other negative experiences of Vietnam deep within under lock and key. They were gone. My second maneuver was "numbing" out, which built secure walls around my life. My third course of action was becoming a workaholic. I poured myself into everything I did, thinking I was doing it all for the right reasons, but unknowingly destroying myself. A fourth tactic was to keep on the move. While in Vietnam my Section was constantly on the move, never staying in the same place for more than a few weeks. I took that home with me and put it to use. Until recently, I have never been in one place for more than five years, except for one eight year period of time.

I met my lovely wife at Northwestern College in Orange City, Iowa back in 1973. We got married in December of 1975. From Iowa we moved to New Jersey to attend Seminary. After one year of schooling we went to Annville, Kentucky for an internship, then back to New Jersey. Upon graduation we served churches in five different States.

Cheryl didn't know what she was getting into when she said, "I do." I eventually dragged her and our family across our Nation from New Jersey to New York. From New York to South Dakota. From South Dakota to Washington State. From Washington back to South Dakota. From South Dakota to Iowa. Then, finally from Iowa to Kentucky, where we have finally settled down.

My journey home from war has been a long one, as have been the journeys of millions of other Veterans down through the centuries. For the most part, we travel it silently in the midst of families and communities. We are present, but gone at the same time. Our hearts and thoughts are with our loved ones, but also with our comrades in arms. In, and through it all, we seek comfort from that which haunts us – war.

Before, during, and after Vietnam I found comfort in God's Word - the Holy Bible.[90] I found solace and relief through prayer.[91] My relationship with Jesus kept me going as He opened each new day with hope and grace.[92] However, my numbing out kept people from building close relationships with me. They always thought they were closer than they actually were. Very few made it through my defenses. Until Cheryl.

I have been blessed with a wonderful God fearing wife who loves Him and me beyond measure. I deserve neither, but am extremely thankful for both. Not all Military personnel and Veterans have it as well as me. Marital breakup and divorce is alarmingly high among Veterans, thus wounding millions more in wars brought home from wars. Countless millions of wounded are still seeking comfort.

Comfort for some came, and still comes, in the form of the bottle or drugs or both. I never got into booze or drugs. I did, however, put myself on self-induced adrenaline highs. But, what went up had to come down. My life was filled with these ups and downs to the point I was harming my body. I did not know that then, but I do now.

Relief from the hauntings of war also came to others in the form of work, like it did for me unknowingly. Some ran from one relationship to another, seeking for something lost. While others simply withdrew from life, bunkering down into an emotional no-mans' zone. The list goes on, as does the list of returning men and women from war.

It is easy to see why some Veterans and Military personnel give up hope of having a normal life among normal people. The truth is, we are different. But, we need not give up in this difference. We need to keep pressing on, seeking the comforting hope that endures through all life's twists & turns and ups & downs.

War haunts many of those who have been or are caught up in its madness. PTSD is such a haunting. It is real. It is all too real for all too many Veterans of all too many wars.

An eighth step to be taken in coming up out of PTSD's deep trench is to allow God's grace to have its perfect way with us[93] in an imperfect world - knowing we can live above fears.

I thank God for the realities of the *"For thou art with me; thy rod and thy staff they comfort me"*[94] of Psalm 23 in wartime and peacetime.

He is truly a proven Comforter as described in Matthew 11:28-30, *"Come to Me, all you who labor and are heavy laden, and I will give you rest. Take My yoke upon you and learn from Me, for I am gentle and lowly in heart, and you will find rest for your souls. My yoke is easy and My burden is light."* And in Romans 15:4, *"For whatever things were written before were written for our learning, that we through the patience and comfort of the Scriptures might have hope."*

Chapter 17

TURNING THE TABLES

Before leaving for Vietnam, my extended family throws a great feast for me. The table is decked out with my favorite foods and desserts. The entire house is filled with the aroma of homemade entrees, freshly baked breads, cakes and pies. We eat, fellowship, hope and pray together into the night. A family table is turned into a community table this day. Through prayer it turns into much more. My family prepares a table before me in the presence of my relatives. In a few short days, my God will prepare a table before me in the presence of my enemies.

I take this memory and hope of my family's table with me to O'Hare Airport, where I say farewell to some who sat around that table with me. These memories, hopes and prayers also fly with me on the various airplanes that take me to Vietnam. Once on the tarmac in Cam Ranh Bay, Vietnam they also depart with me from the plane. From there they follow me throughout my tour. They also are awaiting me, at a gathering of family and relatives on vacation in Wisconsin, upon my return from war.

I never sit at a table draped with a tablecloth while in Vietnam. In fact, our crew members very seldom have the privilege of sitting on chairs around tables, eating wholesome meals in real mess halls serving real food on real plates. When we do, we savor every moment and leave stuffed.

It's amazing what we take for granted. I have never taken water for granted after Vietnam. Nor have I made it a practice of wasting food. Above all, I strive not to take my family nor God for granted.

We Duster crews have it made while on a larger LZ or firebase, because we are supposed to be fed what the Troops, Marines or Airmen are served. And we are not supposed to pull KP. While our Section is pulling perimeter guard on such an LZ, we are denied the privilege of eating in their mess-hall. It is agonizing sitting by our Dusters eating C-rations, knowing everybody else is eating hot meals, pastries and pies. It is excruciating having the aroma filled breeze drift our way from the mess-hall while we are stuck eating our C-rations.

Finally, Chief has enough of the breach of contract and approaches the compound's Commanding Officer about it. The Officer brushes him off, which ticks Chief off. Chief then comes back to our bunker and calls our Battery Commander to inform him of the situation. Chief is told to pack up our Dusters and vacate the LZ. It sounds good to us, and is easy to follow our orders.

We pack up our meager belongings and gather our equipment and load them in our trailer. Then we mount our Tracks and rumble through the LZ to leave through the gate. The Commanding Officer of the LZ frantically runs toward our Dusters as we approach the gate, yelling at us over our roaring engines. We stop shy of the gate to listen to this agitated Officer. Chief dismounts his Track to encounter the Officer, who demands to know what we think we are doing. Chief (David) informs him of our orders and what brought them about. The red-faced Officer apologizes, and we eat well thereafter while on this LZ. The tables are turned in our favor.

After one long day of escort duty, our Section is radioed to travel beyond our destination and travel to a firebase that needs our firepower. We are told we will not be placed in towers since that will be a breach of contract. Duster crews are only to pull guard duty on our Tracks, or our personal guard bunkers – never in guard-towers.

We obey our orders to our own danger, in that we are traveling during dusk, which makes us vulnerable to ambush. We push on making it to the firebase just before nightfall. Once on the firebase, we are ordered by its C.O. to hit the towers. (We were lied to.)We are exhausted. We are mad. But it doesn't matter. The tables are turned against us. We are glad to eventually leave this place.

One night in December of 1970, LZ English is hit hard. It has the makings of being our last night. The bombardment and exchange is fierce. Thankfully, Charlie never makes it to our perimeter wire. The table is turned in our favor.

One never gets ones' way in war, it is out of one's hands. You take what comes your way and press on until your time is up, one way or the other. Even after war – one must press on beyond that war. War has a way of warring on.

War haunts many of those who have been or are caught up in its madness. PTSD is such a haunting. It is real. It is all too real for all too many Veterans of all too many wars.

A ninth step to be taken in coming up out of PTSD's deep trench is to accept the Lord's invitation to His table,[95] rather than making excuses for turning down His gracious invitation.[96]

I thank God for the realities of the "*Thou preparest a table before me in the presence of my enemies*"[97] of Psalm 23 in wartime and peacetime.

He is truly a proven Host of a glorious feast as described in Luke 14:15-24, wherein He says, "*Come, for all things are now ready.*"

Chapter 18

ANOINTING

Feelings, emotions and thoughts are interwoven in the living fabric of human life. I remember these three being hyper - sensitive at a Sunday night worship service in my home church, a few days before my departure for Vietnam. I am surrounded by church and extended family members, some of whom are Veterans.

During the worship service I am "anointed in prayer," which moves me deeply. At the service's closing, I am "anointed in music" when the congregation sings "*God Be With You*."[98] After the service I am "anointed in fellowship." This is followed the next day by an "anointing in advice" from one of my youth sponsors who recently returned from Vietnam. He invites me out for lunch at a restaurant and wisely advises me as a friend, sponsor and Veteran. I take it to heart and leave hopeful.

Feelings, emotions and thoughts are tightly woven in the hearts & lives of a small band of family, relatives and friends in O'Hare's terminal as we wait for my flight. Just before boarding, I am "anointed in hugs, kisses and handshakes." I leave my small band of family members in Chicago, soon to be adopted into an even smaller band of brothers in Vietnam.

Once on the plane I am not alone, for all my "anointings" and my God are with me. My next stop is California, where I am herded into a large staging area with hundreds of other Vietnam bound Troops - of whom I know none. From here I board an airplane for Vietnam, with a short layover in Japan. My flight is about seventeen hours. Seventeen hours of feelings, emotions and thoughts interwoven with faith, hope and prayer.

Many of us went to Vietnam alone. Once there, we were placed in Units as replacements. As replacements, we had to earn our way into acceptance due to trust issues. Could we be trusted under fire? Could we hold up under extremely hostile conditions? Could we keep another persons' back at the expense of our own? We were called "Cherries" until "baptized by fire" – experiencing and surviving enemy fire.

Some people go through their entire war experience never being baptized by fire. They are still there - they are still serving their Country. In actuality, far less than fifty percent of Military personnel are in combat. It takes a lot of personnel and material and effort to keep those who are functioning properly. The effects of war can still touch those who do not experience any form of combat - because war is still war. It wraps it ugly tentacles around anyone anywhere anytime it can. Some can break free from its ungodly grip, while others cannot.

It isn't very long after arriving in Vietnam that I am baptized by fire. My baptism sakes me like a tree's leaf in a windstorm. It chews me up and spits me out like a wad of chewed up gum. It however does not chop me down in defeat. Through God's strength,[99] and my crews' comradeship, I survive it and much more.

The days are long and the nights even longer while serving on a small firebase. There are less than fifty of us within its perimeter. We have no bunkers or guard towers or wooden structures. However, we have each other and each other's backs. There are four Dusters on this small base in a much contested area. For the most part Charlie leaves us alone because of this. But one day we receive word that the NVA are on the move and coming our way.

We are also told to hold at all cost. Suddenly the prospects of a long night get even longer and deadlier.

No one sleeps this night as we all prepare for the worst of the worst. We will be far outnumbered with nowhere to go but to stay put. All four Duster crews remain on high alert all night, manning our Tracks. Gazing into the darkness of night in the darkness of war. Listening intently for any sounds out of place. Enduring the chill of the night while hoping the heat of combat will not come. We face the fact some of us might not come through this alive. We have our orders. We hold our ground. Morning eventually comes, and with it hope for another day.

The NVA bypass us. Facing four Dusters and two 105mm Howitzers might have been too costly for them. Or was the good hand of God upon us,[100] mercifully sparing us and them?

We eventually leave here for LZ English, to handle perimeter duty by night and escorting convoys by day. It is a larger and more secure area, which means we can let our guard down a bit while on the LZ itself. It is during one of these down times, that I am drawn to meditating on Ezra 7:6 pertaining to my prayer life. It is a reassuring time for me as I think on Ezra's prayer life, especially upon the sentence, *"The king granted him all his request, according to the hand of the Lord his God upon him."*

The "hand of God"[101] is another form of anointing. It is one often overlooked and chalked up as good luck or fortune. "God get me through this and I will …" has been on the lips of countless combatants down through the centuries. It has also been forgotten by many once safely brought through their ordeals. Thank God He is patient.[102] However, there is a limit to His patience – it is called time. We cannot outlive God as we all have an appointed time to die.[103] We must take care of business with Him before our time runs out.[104] I wrote upon my boonie hat, "I'm a going home – heaven or Chicago." I hoped for Chicago, but was prepared for heaven. My boonie hat made it through

Vietnam as did I, but to my misfortune it was stolen while I was in college. I miss that hat.

War haunts many of those who have been or are caught up in its madness. PTSD is such a haunting. It is real. It is all too real for all too many Veterans of all too many wars.

A tenth step to be taken in coming up out of PTSD's deep trench is to seek after the Lord's anointing[105] and fulfill our promises to Him.[106]

I thank God for the realities of the *"thou anointest my head with oil,"*[107] of Psalm 23 in wartime and in peacetime.

He is truly a proven Anointer of blessing, as described in Psalm 20:6, *"Now I know the Lord saves His anointed; He will answer him from His holy heaven with the saving strength of His right hand."*

Chapter 19

OVERFLOWING VERSUS STAGNATION

I loathed Vietnam's monsoon season, during which there was no escape from its misery for us Duster crews. Day after day, and night after night, its miserable weather relentlessly pursued us. As bad as we had it, the Infantrymen out in the jungles and rice paddies had it far worse than us. No matter how bad off a person is, there is always someone worse off – especially in wars.

We slushed through endless muddy puddles to get to our Duster. Our boots were forever wet as were our clothes. Our jungle boots, made of canvas & leather, had small screened holes in them through which water squirted out as we walked. And of course our boots, socks, fatigues, underwear, field jacket, flak jacket, helmet, poncho-liner, towels, and all other government issued stuff were Army olive drab green. We were green clad creatures in a war-torn country of endless shades of greens.

Our Section is on a mountaintop firebase for a short while in early December. It is a pitiful place. In fact we eat our C-rations in a bomb crater we call "the pit." We have no bunkers, but do have small two-man shelters made of sandbagged covered culvert halves. One day, a wonderful thing happens to me at the pit that brings a touch of heaven to me and my crew. I receive a large care package from back home. Suddenly, this stagnate place overflows with blessings as I share my bounty with my fellow crew members. My cup of goodies is overflowing.

A week later, we are relocated to LZ English, from which we escort Combat Engineers out to their isolated worksites. It is here that another crew member receives a care package from his family back in the real world. As is the custom, he gets first pick of the goodies, after which he divides some of the remaining blessings with us. I receive a monstrously large red and white candy cane stick, which I slobber over for weeks. One of my crew members takes a picture of me with it - which I still have to this day. The photograph reveals everything about our meager existence at this time, in this place. I am covered with caked on dust, wearing my dingy green jungle fatigues, sitting on top of a dirt covered OD green Duster, clasping a bright red & white candy cane. It isn't much, but it sure is sweet and tasty in a sour place. My cup of sweets is overflowing.

One particular day of escort duty becomes like none other. We are escorting a South Korean Artillery Unit when we are forced to stop, not by enemy fire - but by rain. It is raining so hard we can hardly see. There happens to be a thatched roof, open walled, Vietnamese market near our location. Chief allows two of us from each Duster to dismount our Tracks to stand under the thatched roof. While standing there, small puddles are forming under us from the rain water dripping off our clothes onto the dirt floor.

Toward the back of the market, elderly Vietnamese women stand around their large flat circular weaved baskets of rice. There are also small bamboo cages of chickens, and larger bamboo cages of pot belly pigs. Small tables stacked with fresh fruits add to the mix.

Moments after our arrival, one woman covers her mouth and points her finger at us. We all look down to see if our flies are open. None are. Soon it becomes obvious she is pointing at me.

By now all the women are giggling and pointing their fingers at me.

Then it dawns on me, they think I am munching a boot string - when actually I am eating a black licorice string. I say, "Hey guys, they think I'm eating my boot string." So I place the half eaten string in my mouth and suck it in like a robin sucks in a worm. The women's reactions are priceless. Their jaws drop - revealing poor teeth and wads of beetle nut chews. This is followed by laughing as red beetle nut juice drips down their chins. I give my comrades some licorice strings to eat, which causes the ladies to howl in laughter and chant something in Vietnamese. My cup of laughter is overflowing.

One night, while two of us are pulling perimeter guard duty on our Duster under a full moon, starlit night, I am caught up in a spirit of prayer. Sitting here with my fellow guard, gazing beyond the wire, I pray silently while listening to nature that surrounds us. While my partner takes a twenty minute break to get water and snacks from our bunker, I lift my arms heavenward and praise the Lord for His lovingkindness and faithfulness.[108] My cup of joy is overflowing.

One day, among 365 days, our Section is on the move. We are flagged down by some Allies, who are under attack from Viet Cong shooting down on them from a mountain. We pull over and our sister Track, "Triple Deuce," returns fire unleashing deadly 40mm projectiles on the ambushers. Within seconds the Viet Cong are taken care of, and we are on our way. Our cup of hope to the ambushed Allies is overflowing.

We are out in the boonies for an extended time, which means we do not receive mail on a regular basis. A week or more passes before we receive mail and our letters for home are picked up. These extended times are hard on us, but even more so for our loved ones back in the real world. One lonely day, on this lonesome outpost, we receive a long awaited mail call brought out to us from our Battery Headquarters. Our names are called off alphabetically as we stand around the jeep that brought our mail. Finally, my name is called and to my delight I receive a stack of letters from family, relatives, friends, and church members. Picking them up I think of Proverbs 25:25, *"As cold water to a weary soul, so is good news from a far country."* My cup of blessing is overflowing.

A sad reality of war is the battle deaths of those entering or nearing the end of their tours/deployments. Hope and life are wiped out while loved ones are waiting for good news from a far war-torn country. Prior to the earlier years of Vietnam, these deaths were followed by telegrams sent to the fallen Military personnel's families - informing them of the deaths.

Suddenly, all that remains are letters and memories. There are all too many bundled up letters tucked away in all too many homes, in all too many countries. There are all too many homes with cups overflowing with sorrow.

I am never wounded in Vietnam, but come close to it various times. It is a miracle. Death pursues me and my crew members, but it never overtakes us. We are thankful for this, as are our families back home. However, towards the end of my tour something starts to fester down deep in my soul. I can't identify it, but I know something is wrong. I eventually take this home with me.

The longer I am home the more intense this festering becomes. It is constantly on my mind. Eventually the truth comes out. I am suffering from survivors' quilt. I try to shake it, but it just clings on tighter. I ty to deny it, but it just reinforces its presence. My cup of pain is overflowing. However, my cup of pain slowly begins emptying after I come to terms with its false guilt.

War haunts many of those who have been or are caught up in its madness. PTSD is such a haunting. It is real. It is all too real for all too many Veterans of all too many wars.

An eleventh step to be taken in coming up out of PTSD's deep trench is to rejoice in the overflowing blessings from our gracious Lord God Almighty.[109]

I thank God for the realities of the *"my cup runneth over"*[110] of Psalm 23 in wartime and peacetime.

He is truly a proven Bearer of wonderful gifts as described in Romans 6:23, *"For the wages of sin is death, but the gift of God is eternal life in Christ Jesus our Lord."* And James 1:17, *"Every good gift and every perfect gift is from above, and comes down from the Father of lights, with whom there is no variation or shadow of turning."*

Chapter 20

GOODNESS & MERCY
GO TO WAR

I am thinking of my childhood days growing up in Chicago while sitting on a bunker. The bunker overlooks a deep valley with a river flowing through it, and lush mountains rising beyond. It is safe for me to do this as there are guards on duty - freeing me to be lost in thought. I never seen such beautiful terrain as I am seeing in the Central Highlands of South Vietnam.

My thoughts go farther back to my elementary school social studies class, where we studied the Vietnam Conflict. Never in my wildest dreams did I dream I'd end up fighting in Vietnam. After graduating from Chicago Vocational High School I enlisted in the Army. I went through Boot Camp and A.I.T. under the false assumption of never being sent to Vietnam, because of being a sole surviving son of my family.

I'll never forget the day I came down on levy for Vietnam, nor will my mother and sisters. It is heart wrenching news for my mother. Such news is still heart wrenching to parents, grandparents, spouses, and children of men and women being sent off to war.

I phoned home, hoping my older sister would answer. To my great relief, Nancy was home and picked up the phone. I asked her if mom was on the other line. Nancy said, "No." After some very brief small talk, I dropped the bomb of my coming down on levy for Vietnam. An agitated voice on the other side of the line said, "You volunteered didn't you?" I said that I didn't, but came down on levy, and that I talked to my First Sergeant about my being a sole surviving son. To which he said that deferment no longer existed. I didn't convince her as she stood trembling, thinking about what was happening and could happen. I told her I was getting a 30 day leave very shortly and would tell Mom face to face within a week.

Unknown to me, my mother picked up the other phone in her bedroom and heard the conversation. She placed her hand over the phone, and her other hand over her heart - gasping for air. When Nancy hanged up the receiver, mom dropped hers and wept bitterly. Nancy tried to comfort her, but such comfort was beyond her ability. As mom wept Nancy's anger grew. They sat on mom's bed, side by side, with shattered hearts. My widowed mother could soon be sonless as well.

Later that night, an orderly approached me in the barrack's bay saying I had a phone call. Now it was my turn to receive unwanted news. Nancy told me mom had been on the other line and heard the news, and took it badly. After our brief conversation, I went back to my locker for a fistful of quarters to fill the public pay phone. I prayed for strength, wisdom and words to share with mom as I dialed my home phone. Nancy answered and told mom it was me. Our conversation, mixed with prayer, lasted longer than my quarters - so I quickly went for more. The operator eventually broke in informing us we only had a minute left. What could be said in a minute? Mom told the operator to reverse the charges, and we continued to talk. We eventually closed in prayer.

That night, mom had to retire to the very room she received the worst news of her life. I do not know if she slept. I imagine every person can remember where they were, and what they were doing, when receiving news of a loved one being sent off to war.

The effects of war has a way of starting before one is sent off to war. Many civilians are clueless about this as they go on their daily routines. Presently, less than one percent of America's eligible aged people are serving in the Military. What percentage of the 99 pray for our Troops and their families? What percentage of the 99 take the less than one percent for granted? What would happen if the less than one percent said, "That's enough," and left the Military?

That fateful night, Grace read and reread Psalm 23, as did I. That Psalm is packed full of comfort and hope. That night I focused in on, *"surely goodness and mercy shall follow me all the days of my life."*[111] God's goodness is good and His mercy is merciful in good and bad times, and those times in between.[112]

I was taught to be good and show goodness to others.[113] I was also taught to show mercy rather than hatred.[114] These qualities would soon be put to the test.

My thirty day leave shot by. So little time to do so much before departing on what could be a one way trip. I remember listening to music a lot. I spent time meditating in the Word and praying. I spent as much time with family, relatives and friends as I could. I found comfort and support in Sunday morning and evening worship services.

Within those thirty days, Nancy came to terms with her anger after realizing I didn't volunteer for Vietnam. Mom tried to come to terms with her fear. It was out of our hands. It was in God's hands. We had to entrust ourselves and each other in His hands and wills for our lives. Mom said, "I trusted God, but my only son was going to Vietnam."

Before the days of cell-phones and email we had to rely upon mail that took a week or more to arrive. Hopefully with messages of hope, goodness and mercy. I would read and reread my mail. In fact, all my Squad members reread their mail. Sometimes, we would even share our letters with each other.

Those practices where customary in the Military, and have been for centuries.

Loved ones back home lived for mail. Daily they hoped to receive letters, for with them came hope that their loved ones were still alive. Day by day they hoped. 365 days was a long time for people living hourly. A good day was a day one received mail. Goodness and mercy came their way from Vietnam (or any war their loved ones were in).

Goodness and mercy followed me to Vietnam and stayed with me the whole time. While in Vietnam I had good and bad days. I had days in which I cried out to God for mercy. I had days in which I shared goodness and mercy with my fellow crew members and other Troops nearby. I had days in which I shared goodness and mercy with the Vietnamese. And I had some days in which I showed mercy towards the Viet Cong.

Goodness and mercy can be strong allies in war, if we let them. On the other hand, in the heat of battle, goodness and mercy can get you killed. Many combatants have to make snap decisions of who lives and dies. These decisions are part of war, but they don't stay there. They come home with those who survive it. Once home, these decisions can turn into unwelcomed dreams, nightmares and flashbacks. They can also turn into hauntings that plague Veterans for decades.

There is much more to war than just war. War, be it justified or not, is a scourge that plagues the human race. We cannot wish it away. It is here to stay. The Bible places the causes of war squarely upon us as described in James 4:1-2; and that we can expect wars and rumors of wars right up to the end of time.[115]

Memories and monuments honoring those who served in wars are important, lest we forget the terrible cost of freedom. But, they are not enough, because they are too easily overlooked or ignored. It all boils down to a heart issue. What is in our hearts eventually works its way out into our thoughts and actions, which work their ways into the lives of others.

I wasn't always a perfect Christian while in Vietnam. Some days were hard to let goodness have its way. In those days I called upon God for mercy.

When thrown into the insanity of combat - goodness and mercy are the last things on your mind. If you lose a fellow comrade - goodness and mercy might be the last things in your heart. If you leave war severely wounded - goodness and mercy for the enemy might be nonexistent. Thus, some combatants leave war angry at God for the lack of goodness and mercy in their lives in their wars.

War haunts many of those who have been or are caught up in its madness. PTSD is such a haunting. It is real. It is all too real for all too many Veterans of all too many wars.

A twelfth step to be taken in coming up out of PTSD's deep trench is to trust God's goodness and mercy at all times in all places.[116]

I thank God for the realities of the *"Surely goodness and mercy shall follow me all the days of my life"*[117] of Psalm 23 in wartime and peacetime.

He is truly a proven Provider of goodness & mercy as described in Psalm 37:13, *"I would have lost heart, unless I had believed that I would see the goodness of the Lord in the land of the living."* And in Ephesians 2:4-5, *"But God who is rich in mercy, because of His great love with which He loved us, even when we were dead in trespasses, made us alive together with Christ (by grace you have been saved)."*

Chapter 21

DWELLING

"Where do I go from here?" is asked by many Troops upon coming home from war. Civilians might simply say, "Go home."

Home sounds nice. Home sounds safe. But is it? To the surprise of civilians the answer often is "no."

War doesn't stay on the battlefield, it often comes home with the returning Troops. Sometimes it is obvious as these men and women start falling into self-destructive behaviors. But, then there are those who are not as obvious, for they suffer in silence. Holding everything in - they live like nothing happened. But, down deep there is something happening, and it's trying to get out. Eventually it does come out to the surprise, and sometimes demise, of relationships with family, friends and coworkers. War finally comes home. Then, there are some very fortunate folks who leave war on the battlefields and live free of its negative effects – hopefully all of their lives.

In September of 1970 I started my count down of days to my departure from Vietnam. Day by day I counted them down. Day by day I lived each one hoping to see the next day. This was done by all Vietnam Veterans and all Veterans since then.

We had tours back then. Today they have deployments. I find it hard to believe that present day Military personnel have multiple deployments of up to three, four, or more. Off to war – come back home. Off to war – come back home. Off to war – come back home. What is this doing to Military families? I know what my one tour of Vietnam did to my mother.

Thinking of home makes one homesick, which makes one's time in war that much harder. On the other hand, not thinking of home can make one delusional. Thinking of home can bring moments of joy and hope in troubling situations. Thinking of home can also bring about camaraderie among those serving in isolated areas. Thinking of home while on guard duty can get one killed, along with others. There is a proper time for thinking of home and there is an improper time for thinking of home. Then there is the wisdom of knowing the difference that comes through time – if one lives long enough.

"Home is where the heart is," is an old saying that is forever new in the lives of those being sent out in harms' way of combat. Once combat erupts, those caught up in its explosive madness empty "home" from their hearts to pour their hearts into killing. Home at this point is their comrades in arms – there is no other home but them. Together they fight to stay alive. Those who survive patch up their family in order to go through it again (and again, and again …).

Combatants leaving their combat families to reenter their families back home often create blended families. These blended families are not with new spouses and adopted children. They are the intermingling of their immediate families with their comrades in arms within their hearts. These new blended families are often misunderstood by loved ones trying to figure out what's happening to their relationships - or lack of it. The bond of sacrificial love created through trust, and tempered by combat, is often stronger than the bond between husband and wife.

I didn't leave Vietnam alone, I brought my crew and Section members with me in my heart and soul. To this day I can still hear their voices and see their faces in my heart. I cherish these memories. To this day I can still see, taste, smell, feel, and hear the times we were in the Duster engaging the enemy. These are bitter – sweet memories.

Life moves on taking with it the past - be it good, bad, indifferent, or all three intertwined together. It is hard to believe over forty years have passed since my tour of Vietnam. Its presence is always present. There is not a day that goes by in which Vietnam escapes me. I am sure I am not alone in this. I am sure this is true of other Veterans of other wars, past and present.

Through much counseling, therapy, prayer, and determination I have made it this far after falling prey to Post Traumatic Stress Disorder (PTSD). Just because I have it, doesn't mean I am giving in to it. My life is defiantly different, but I do my best to make the best of it. It takes a lot of work and determination to press on. But, life is worth the living – even with PTSD.

It was not easy for my family at first, nor for me. My wife was reduced to fears and tears. My daughters' hearts were broken, and they nearly moved out to find peace and release from the emotional pain I was causing them. Our loving home that sustained us for decades became a prison in which my family felt trapped. Something had to give before the golden cord of love that held us together started to unravel and snap. For me, that something was admitting I had a problem and had to deal with it. That "dealing with it" was calling the VA for help, which eventually ended up with me being admitted into the six week clinical in-house PTSD Rehabilitation Program. For six weeks the Lexington, Kentucky VA Hospital became my home away from home.

Thankfully, that golden cord of love held strong, reassuring us that our family was still a family and always would be. But, what a ride through uncharted emotional terrain that was for us. We read stories about such trips, never thinking we would eventually have a reservation for our own.

Coming home from war involves much more than just coming home from war. It is giving up one way of life for another. What? One no longer has to kill to stay alive. One no longer has to be hyper vigilant to maintain safety. One no longer has to sleep with a loaded weapon to fight off enemy. One no longer has to live in fear of being thrown into conflict in a minute's notice. One no longer has to pull guard duty two or three times a night. One no longer has to look for traps cleverly laid out by the enemy. One no longer has to be hard core emotionally to maintain sanity. But we do. Why? War is hard to break.

Some Veterans are able to break free from some of these things, while other Veterans drag them along until death do they part. The cost of war is costly, especially to families. And what makes up communities – families. And what makes up countries – communities. A sad statistic of combat Veterans is the high divorce rate. One Veteran – multiple families that have multiple families.

Some men and women feel forsaken by God while enduring the harsh realities of combat. Where is God? How can God allow this to happen? Does God even care what's happening to me?

These and other unanswered questions lead to bitterness toward God and toward the Church that represents Him. "I lost my religion while in war" has been said by Veterans down through the ages. It is another way of saying, "I no longer trust God."

Thus, when such men and women should be opening their heart's doors to the Lord,[118] they nail them shut or secure them from within with deadbolts. Time after time they hear the Lord knocking, but ignore His presence. Eventually, His knocking is pushed out of mind like a slow dripping faucet in a basement sink. It can wait until I get around to it, if I ever do.

War haunts many of those who have been or are caught up in its madness. PTSD is such a haunting. It is real. It is all too real for all too many Veterans of all too many wars.

A thirteenth step to be taken in coming up out of PTSD's deep trench is abiding in the Lord within the House of the Lord,[119] in which there is hope, comfort and strength.[120]

I thank God for the realities of the "*I will dwell in the house of the Lord for ever*"[121] of Psalm 23 in wartime and peacetime.

He is truly a proven secure dwelling place as described in Psalm 91:1-2, "*He who dwells in the secret place of the Most High shall abide under the shadow of the Almighty. I will say of the Lord, 'He is my refuge and my fortress; my God in Him I will trust.'*"

CONCLUSION

Life is filled with journeys, of which you are on one by reading <u>PTSD & PSALM 23: Coming Up Out Of PTSD's Trench</u>. Your journey is not finished, but only beginning as you apply the previous thirteen steps. Press forward one day at a time in them - remembering PTSD will be part of your life all your life. This however does not need to drag you down. It can actually lift you up. Your time in the Service was (is) not in vain, nor is your life today. Life is worth the living.

Here is a spiritual roadmap for **JOURNEY**:

Joy is a joyous thing when it is allowed to have its rightful place in your life.[122]

Opening your heart to the Lord rather than closing it opens new paths to blessings.

Understanding what is happening in your life is important for a healthy mind & life.

Realize God moves in mysterious ways to get you where you need to be.

Never give in to PTSD, but fight it for yourself and for others who need you.

Entertain God's Word in your daily life for strength, direction and hope.[123]

Yearn to learn what God is trying to teach you. Because your life has purpose.[124]

As a child growing up in Chicago, my father received one week of vacation, which he used to take our family up to Wisconsin for visiting relatives. When he finally received two weeks we still went up to Wisconsin to visit relatives, but we also joined additional relatives staying in rental cabins. I have a lifetime of memories of fishing with my father & uncles & by myself, of swimming & waterskiing, of playing games with my cousins, and of sitting around camp fires roasting marshmallows.

I can remember with fondness counting down the months, then weeks, then days to our departure date for our annual journey. I remember the week prior of soaking the back yard so we could hunt night crawlers after nightfall. It was a learned skill that took much patience as I had to learn to walk softly, move slowly, hold a flashlight in one hand and try to catch a worm with the other. Once caught, we placed them into a coffee can filled with used coffee grounds & dirt. Afterwards, we put a lid on it with puncture holes so our bait could live.

The morning of our departure my dad took his time loading the car as I paced around wishing he'd hurry. My sisters had their stuff neatly on the floor in front of them and next to them on the seat, until I jumped into the car to claim my rightful place. The backseat battle began.

It was a long hot journey before interstates and air conditioning. I remember thinking how strange it was beyond the city limits. The ride itself was an escapade of sights and sounds as we traveled northward on two lane country roads. Looking out the window I saw long black drooping telephone lines that rose and lowered as telephone poles swooshed by. I heard the endless whistle of air passing through the front breeze windows, and the humming of our tires on the road. I also heard my sisters' battle cries to my constant attempts of claiming more space. I tried to ignore my parents constantly calling out my name. Why me? There were two girls back here too!

Those days are long gone, but not forgotten. They are precious to me, along with many other childhood memories. Then there are the memories of Vietnam, which are just as vivid today as their happenings were way back then. There are also marriage and family memories that span forty years which I treasure. Through all these memories is the intertwined cord of faith, hope and love[125] that gives meaning to all of them.

Life does not happen in a vacuum, even if we try to isolate ourselves. Life has a way of finding us wherever we are, because God is its creator.[126] As Creator He knows what is best for us,[127] and can recreate us through His Son,[128] and set us on a new path in life.[129]

In conclusion, there is a fourteenth step to be taken in coming up out of PTSD's deep trench, which is to continue pressing forward even if we stumble on the way - knowing the Lord is there for us.[130]

He is truly a proven Companion who will never forsake nor leave us as described in John 6:37-40, and in Isaiah 41:10, *"Fear not, for I am with you; be not dismayed, for I am your God. I will strengthen you, yes, I will help you, I will uphold you with My righteous right hand."*

SCRIPTURAL REFERENCES

INTRODUCTION

[1] 1 Peter 1:22-25; 1 John 4:7; Ephesian 5:25; Colossians 5:18-21; Psalm 31:14; Proverbs 3:5-6; Jerimiah 17:7-8.

[2] 1 Corinthians 13:15; Romans 5:1-2; Lamentations 3:5-27; Colossians 2:2-3; 1 John 4:11.

NIGHT

[3] Romans 12:12; Ephesians 6:18; Jude 20-212; Timothy 3:16–17; Psalm 3:4–5; Psalm 119: Joshua 1:8–9.

[4] Psalm 124:7–8.

[5] Hebrews 4:12–13; 2 Timothy 2:15; 1 John 4:18.

[6] Philippians 4:6-7; 2 Thessalonians 3:3; Matthew 24:42; Matthew 26:41; 1 Corinthians 16:13-14.

[7] 2 Timothy 2:17; Joshua 1:9.

[8] Psalm 42:8; Psalm 63:6-8.

GUARD DUTY

[9] Psalm 42:5-11; Psalm 43:5; Mark 9:24; Hebrews 4:14-16.

[10] Philippians 4:6-7; 1 Thessalonians 5:16-18; & 5:23-24.

[11] Proverbs 14:27; Matthew 6:25-34.

[12] 1 Timothy 6:13.

[13] Ephesians 6:17; Hebrews 4:12.

[14] Psalm 46:10.

[15] Deuteronomy 31:8.

[16] Psalm 18:35; Psalm 31:14-15.

17 Psalm 100:4.

18 Psalm 14:26-27; Matthew 6:25-34; 1 Timothy 6:11-16.

19 Ephesians 6:10-13; Romans 13:11-14.

20 Matthew 8:7; Proverbs 10:16; John 8:34; Romans 6:23.

SLEEP

21 Heidelberg Catechism (written in 1563) it contains questions & answers pertaining the Lord's Prayer & the Ten Commandments & the Apostles' Creed.

22 Joshua 1:9.

DASHED HOPES

23 Psalm 147:3; Isaiah 61:1; Luke 4:18-22.

24 James 1:2-5; 1 Peter 1:6-9; Matthew 5:11-12; Romans 5:3-4.

25 Proverbs 23:18; Romans 5:1-2.

26 Hebrews 5:17-20.

MOUNTING UP

27 Luke 9:23; Matthew 6:11.

28 Matthew 6:25-34.

29 Ester 4:13-14; Nehemiah 1:4-11.

REPEAT

30 Romans 5:5; Psalm 37:6.

31 Isaiah 52:126; 2 Thessalonians 3:3.

32 2 Thessalonians 33.

IT'S OFFICIAL

33 Exodus 34:6-7; 2 Corinthians 1:3-4.

34 2 Corinthians 12:9; Psalm 84:10-11.

35 2 Thessalonians 2:16-17.

36 Psalm 13:5-6; 1 Chronicles 16:34; Psalm 52:8-9.

37 Luke 18:1-5; 1 Thessalonians 5:17; Ephesians 6:18.

[38]   Ecclesiastes 3:8.

EXPENDABLE

[39]   Genesis 1:26-27; Genesis 5:1-2.

[40]   2 Samuel 11:1-4.

[41]   2 Samuel 11:5.

[42]   2 Samuel 11:6-13.

[43]   2 Samuel 11:14-17.

[44]   2 Samuel 12:1-13.

GUARDIAN

[45]   Psalm 23:1.

[46]   James 4:7-8.

[47]   Psalm 23:1 (KJV).

[48]   Psalm 119:117; Proverbs 29:25.

G.I. WANT?

[49]   Psalm 39:7; Psalm 38:15-16; Colossians 1:27; Hebrews 6:17-18.

RELAXATION: WHAT'S THAT?

[50]   Philippians 4:6-7; Philippians 1:19-21.

[51]   Psalm 23:2 (KJV).

[52]   Psalm 23:2 (KJV).

WATER

[53]   Psalm 23:2 (KJV).

[54]   Psalm 23:2 (KJV).

[55]   Ephesians 2:14-16.

[56]   Philippians 4:6-7; John 14:27.

[57]   John 7:37-38; John 4:10; Isaiah 12:2-3.

[58]   Isaiah 12:1-3.

[59]   Isaiah 44:3.

[60]   Psalm 23:2 (KJV).

RESTORATION
[61] Job 30:26; Proverbs 15:3; Psalm 37:27-29; Amos 5:14; Romans 12:9-21.
[62] Philippians 4:8.
[63] Ecclesiastes 3:8.
[64] Galatians 5:22-26; Hebrews 12:3; Galatians 5:19-21.
[65] Ecclesiastes 3:7.
[66] Ecclesiastes 3:1-8.
[67] Psalm 119:147.
[68] John 10:27-30.
[69] 1 Samuel 16:7; 1 Kings 8:39; Psalm 139:23-24.
[70] Luke 12:4-7.
[71] Genesis 1:26.
[72] Psalm 23:3 (KJV).
[73] Psalm 139:7-10; Isaiah 41:13.

LEADING ME, OR LEADING ME ON
[74] 1 Corinthians 16:34; Luke 18:9-14; Psalm 13:5-6.
[75] Psalm 23:3 (KJV).
[76] Ephesians 2:8-10.
[77] Psalm 23:4.
[78] Psalm 145:14; James 4:10; Psalm 30:1-3; Psalm 114:7.
[79] 1 John 1:7; 1 Corinthians 6:11.
[80] Colossians 1:1-3; Numbers 6: 24-26.
[81] Psalm 31:3.
[82] Matthew 7:13-14.
[83] Matthew 20:16.
[84] Psalm 23:3 (KJV).

DEATH
[85] 1 Timothy 6:16.
[86] Psalm 23:4.
[87] Isaiah 9:6; Ephesians 2:14.

[88] Joshua 1:7; Romans 8:31-39; 2 Timothy 1"7; 1 John 4:18.

[89] Psalm 23:4 (KJV).

COMFORT

[90] 1 Thessalonians 4:11.

[91] 1 Peter 4:7-9; Matthew 6:5-15; Philippians 4:6-7.

[92] Lamentations 3:23-24.

[93] 2 Corinthians 1:22-24.

[94] Psalm 234 (KJV).

TURNING THE TABLES

[95] Luke 16:17.

[96] Luke 14:18-20.

[97] Psalm 23:4 (KJV).

[98] Words by Jeremiah E. Richards 1880; Music composed by John W. Bichoff; written as a Christian good – by.

[99] 2 Samuel 22:2-3; Psalm 46:1; Jeramiah 16:19; Philippians 4:13.

[100] Ezra 7:6.

[101] Ezra 7:6 & 28; 1 Peter 5:6-7.

[102] Romans 5:5-6.

[103] Hebrews 9:27-28; Psalm 9:12.

[104] 2 Corinthians 5:10; Proverbs 8:17; John 3:18-21.

[105] 2 Corinthians 1:21-22; Ephesians 4:30-32.

[106] Ecclesiastes 5:4-5.

[107] Psalm 23:5 (KJV).

OVERFLOWING VERSUS STAGNATION

[108] Psalm 63:3-5; Lamentations 3:22-24; Hosea 3:19-20; Jonah 4:2.

[109] Ephesians 1:3-6.

[110] Psalm 23:5 (KJV).

GOODNESS & MERCY GO TO WAR

[111] Psalm 23:6.

[112] 1 Peter 5:6-7.

[113] Isaiah 1:16-18; Romans 12: 20-21; Hebrews 10:23-25.

[114] Micah 6:8; Matthew 5:7.

[115] Mark 13:7-8.

[116] Psalm 52:1; Genesis 34:6-7; 1 Chronicles 34: 6-7; Psalm 106:1.

[117] Psalm 23:6 (KJV).

DWELLING

[118] Colossians 3:15.

[119] Psalm 27:4-5.

[120] Galatians 6:6-10; Romans 12:9-21; 1 Peter 2:4-5.

[121] Psalm 23:6 (KJV).

CONCLUSION

[122] Nehemiah 8:10; John 15:9-17; Romans 15:13; Romans 14:17-18.

[123] Philippians 4:8-9; 2 Timothy 2:15; Joshua 1:8-9; Psalm 119:97.

[124] Matthew 11:28-30; Romans 15:4; Philippians 4:11-13; Isaiah 1:16-17.

[125] 1 Corinthians 13:13.

[126] Genesis 1:26-28; Genesis 5:1-2 Mark 10:5-9.

[127] Psalm 51: 5-10.

[128] 2 Corinthians 5:17.

[129] Proverbs 3:5-6.

[130] Psalm 37:17; Psalm 63:8-9; Psalm 145:14.

CPSIA information can be obtained
at www.ICGtesting.com
Printed in the USA
LVOW12s1452080917

548055LV00001B/17/P